ENDORSEMENTS

Bill Johnson has been a friend of years ever since I made a point of seeking to know the relative substance of his ministry and mindset. Through doing what many do (i.e. question his ministry worth while criticizing it), I sought to make acquaintance with him. I wanted to know the man—to know the relative depth of his biblical grounds for ministry and personal character in conducting that ministry.

Everything I have come to know of Bill demonstrates to my view a faithful shepherd, faithfully nurturing a local flock from that base evolving into a functional congregation and providing a valid evidence and worth of his ministry.

With comfort and confidence, I believe reading his writings will contribute to the understanding and growth of believers who open to and welcome the vital functional ministry of Jesus Himself to flow into and through them.

JACK W. HAYFORD
Chancellor Emeritus
The King's University
Southlake, Texas

I just received Bill Johnson's new book, *The Way of Life*, from the publisher. I sat down and read the book, amazed by the wisdom related to living life not only as a husband, father, and Christian, but also as a pastor or leader in the church, as well as in the Kingdom of God. I loved the book—found it full of amazing insights from the Bible and from Bill's experience in living out biblical principles in his various roles. The wisdom in the book makes it an appropriate gift for saint and sinner alike. The beauty and the wisdom of the way to live life presented should attract everyone to the Savior and Empowerer of our lives. This is truly a book that everyone needs to read. I found it valuable as a guide for not only our nuclear families, but also a guide for our church families or congregations.

RANDY CLARK, D.MIN.
Overseer of the Apostolic Network of Global Awakening
Founder of Global Awakening
Bestselling author of *There is More; Power to Heal;* and coauthor of
Essential Guide to Healing with Bill Johnson

A lifestyle of miracles, hearing God's voice, answered prayer, supernatural breakthrough, and fruitfulness is available—now! It's not for some elite status of super Christians who minister from global pulpits or preach in large crusades. As you read this book, you will discover how to actually access and walk in the supernatural way of life that Jesus promised was available!

MARK BATTERSON
Lead Pastor of National Community Church
The New York Times bestselling author of *The Circle Maker*

I start each television show by saying, "Welcome to my world where it's naturally supernatural!" Now Bill Johnson, in this signature book, teaches how you can be normal—normal based on the Bible!

SID ROTH
Host, *"It's Supernatural!"*

I couldn't even get through reading the first chapter of *The Way of Life* without being deeply impacted with an invitation to surrender to God in greater levels than I have ever walked in previously. This book will fill and empower every heart who desires God to be everything to them—and for those who don't identify with that desire, you will after reading this book. I know no one who consistently models this message more than Bill Johnson. He not only communicates the message, he lives the message, he imparts the message. Thank you, Bill Johnson, for being *you* and for freely sharing with all of us the wisdom you have learned through your life of surrender to Christ.

PATRICIA KING
Patricia King Ministries

In each generation leaders arise who carry a message and mandate that literally shifts the course of the particular generation. Bill Johnson is unquestionably such a leader. He has supernaturally established a church and global ministry that has become the epicenter of the modern revival movement. The constant question is, "How?" In this book, Bill answers that question with humility, honesty, and grace. He teaches you how to live a supernatural lifestyle and carry the flames of revival daily. This writing will stoke your passion for more while settling your heart deep into the Father's love and pleasure for your life.

RYAN LeSTRANGE
Founder RLM,TRIBE, iHubs, and TRIBE Books/Media
Author of *Hell's Toxic Trio*

Recently I was given a detailed dream concerning the necessity of being a Values-Based Believer in the days in which we live and the days that are coming. Bill and Beni Johnson are people who live their lives from Heart Core Values. We make big and small decisions, set short and long-range goals from the compass of our heart. Bill's values have impacted my life and are impacting an entire generation around the world. This might be the most significant book Bill Johnson has penned since *When Heaven Invades Earth*.

JAMES W. GOLL
Founder of God Encounters Ministries
GOLL Ideation LLC
Bestselling author of *The Seer; Dream Language;* and *The Discerner*

I have known Bill Johnson for more than forty years. In that time, I never met a Christian more open to obeying Jesus. In *The Way of Life*, he sums up the message of his life. Here you will inherit the two truths that terrify satan most: that revival should be permanent, and that just having Jesus is inexpressibly wonderful.

MARIO MURILLO
Evangelist
Bestselling author of *Fresh Fire* and *Reaching Critical Mass*

The Way of Life by Bill Johnson, what an incredible gift! This book is a treasury of divine wisdom. It's a banqueting table full of insight, revelation, and divine strategy on experiencing the supernatural as a natural way of life. I believe this book carries such an impartation for greater awakening to all that has been given to us in Jesus, walking in the finished work of the Cross in greater ways, and partnering with the Holy Spirit to see transformation. I believe as you feast on the treasures of revelation from the word that Bill shares, along with his personal experience with the Holy Spirit and keys to stewarding the supernatural lifestyle, you will not only encounter Jesus in a deeper way but also be positioned to partner with Him in greater ways to see radical transformation wherever He leads you. I believe the fire of His presence will ignite a greater hunger and faith within you as you read these pages to experience the supernatural as a natural way of life! Get ready for a feast that will change your life! It sure did mine!

LANA VAWSER
Speaker, Prophetic Voice
Author of *The Prophetic Voice of God*
lanavawser.com
Sunshine Coast, Australia

Bill Johnson is a dear friend who we have walked with for close to two decades. He is one of my favorite theologians. He is constantly seeking God for deeper revelation into the Scriptures with the motivation to inspire others to know God's character and their potential in God. In his book *The Way of Life*, Bill teaches us about shaping culture by partnering with Holy Spirit, knowing who we are in Christ, and walking in the supernatural. Each one of us can be the catalyst for transformation in our community, or wherever He leads. The Way of Life helps us discover who we are in Christ. We are His shining ones.

HEIDI G. BAKER, PhD
Cofounder and CEO of Iris Global
Best-selling author of *Birthing the Miraculous*

"Peace is the oxygen of Heaven..." The revelation of this one Kingdom concept alone is worth picking up and studying Bill

Johnson's latest book, *The Way of Life*. Discovering the fullness of this way—applying the principles of this way found in these pages—will revolutionize first your mind, then your faith, next your spirit, and ultimately your entire life. Breakthrough is your portion and this book paves the way to a life of spiritual breakthrough as the gateway for every other breakthrough you'll ever need. Bill has written many impactful books over the years, but this one may be the all-encompassing inspiration you need to walk in your highest life while you advance Christ's agenda on the earth.

JENNIFER LECLAIRE
Senior Leader, Awakening House of Prayer
Founder, Ignite prophetic network
Bestselling author of *Mornings with the Holy Spirit* and *Dream Wild*

Bill Johnson lives life simply through his intimacy with God. When you read his *The Way of Life,* each page illuminates valuable lessons learned and noteworthy revelations received as a disciple and student of His Presence. He truly values the journey to growing in character and trust in our ever-faithful God. The impact of developing through deeper intimacy with God releases an empowering influence that supernaturally shifts the atmosphere to bring forth revival and transformation in families, communities, and connections worldwide. I believe that you will gain powerful, life-giving insights into genuinely abiding in Him personally and interactively to affect our world tremendously. Receive increase in faith and wisdom for your life experiences as you heed the rich perspective of Bill Johnson, my covenant revival brother.

CHÉ AHN
President & Founder, Harvest International Ministry
International Chancellor, Wagner University

Bill Johnson's *The Way of Life's* subtitle should be *Let's free you from any false programming and come into clarity of heart, mind, and spirit.* I feel that he takes the reader through a course in authentic Christianity. Sharing from his own experiences, he teaches us to understand what the way of life is and what the way of life is not.

There are so many profound statements to highlight, think about, meditate on, and go deep into; but when you put the whole book into perspective, this is the kind of Christianity the world needs to be introduced to. It's so empowering and so encouraging, I found myself reading certain sections over and over, like one might do with the book of Proverbs, just to make sure it was going into me. I highly recommend this book!

SHAWN BOLZ
www.bolzministries.com
Author of *Translating God, God Secrets,*
and *Keys to Heaven's Economy*
Host of *Exploring the Prophetic* Podcast

This book contains extensive revelation that equips the reader with potent tools to living a supernatural lifestyle. I want to personally endorse and recommend this book by Bill Johnson. The insight and revelation in this book will change your perspective on life and how you live it.

The supernatural realm is a way of Kingdom living. Supernatural living breaks limitations and barriers of our mind. Prepare yourself as you read this book to be challenged and stretched.

I pray that as you read this book that God will give you understanding in all things. Step into this realm and live the supernatural lifestyle that God desires for you to live. Don't be afraid of this realm. Embrace it and rejoice in its benefits.

John Eckhardt
Bestselling author of *Prayers That Rout Demons*

THE

WAY

of

LIFE

DESTINY IMAGE BOOKS BY BILL JOHNSON

BILL JOHNSON

THE

WAY

of

LIFE

EXPERIENCING
THE CULTURE OF
HEAVEN ON EARTH

DESTINY IMAGE® PUBLISHERS, INC.

P.O. Box 310, Shippensburg, PA 17257-0310

"Promoting Inspired Lives."

This book and all other Destiny Image and Destiny Image Fiction books are available at Christian bookstores and distributors worldwide.

Cover design by Christian Rafetto
Interior design by Terry Clifton

For more information on foreign distributors, call 717-532-3040.

Reach us on the Internet: www.destinyimage.com.

ISBN 13: 978-0-7684-4272-4
ISBN 13 eBook: 978-0-7684-4273-1
ISBN 13 Large Print: 978-0-7684-4808-5
ISBN 13 International TP: 978-0-7684-4274-8

For Worldwide Distribution, Printed in the U.S.A.
1 2 3 4 5 6 7 8 / 22 21 20 19 18

DEDICATION

I dedicate this book to my city, its region, and the people who live here. Redding means salvation in Dutch. And it has the Sacramento River flowing through the middle of town, which of course refers to *the river of sacrament*. Our cry is that the faithful men and women who serve our city with purity, power, and vision would represent Jesus well, and bring about the transformation that most brings Him glory. Redding, and the surrounding region, is better off today because of your love and devotion. And whether you serve in business, politics, education, medicine, media, as a stay at home mom, pastoring a church, or some other beautiful role of service, the effect of your life is priceless. I have no doubt that a Reformation has begun. Let our cry be the same as the Moravians, "May the Lamb that was slain receive the reward of His suffering!"

ACKNOWLEDGMENTS

Many thanks go to Pam Spinosi, who once again helped me to put the final product together. Your editing and counsel was a lifesaver.

Thanks also to Dann Farrelly, who examines my material with a keen eye, helping me to communicate my heart with much greater clarity. Thanks as well for permission to use a piece from *Kingdom Culture*.

Much thanks goes to Michael Van Tinteren and Abigail McKoy for your tireless service in helping me with all things, but especially in this case—completing my writing assignments.

I also want to thank Larry Sparks of Destiny Image Publishing for the excellence and encouragement he brings to my life and writing.

Special thanks also go to Dale Harrison, a dear friend and partner in ministry. He came to my office several years ago and stated something to the effect of, "You don't realize how different things are here at Bethel. You need to write about it." I couldn't shake his words, until finally *The Way of Life* was written.

For me to prepare my heart means that I come to Him in adoration first. I don't come with a need for a message. I come in adoration out of desire to be with Him. And I would rather have nothing to say and be current in my fellowship with Him than to have lots to say and be trying to find Him. That's the main thing for me—I make sure that I am current...that my relationship is fresh. It's about feeling His pleasure, which is the awareness of His heart.

CONTENTS

FOREWORD

by John Bevere

I have the privilege of calling Pastor Bill Johnson my friend. Our times together are always rich, due to his intimate relationship with the Holy Spirit, deep knowledge of the Word of God, and—most outstanding—his genuine humility.

Bill, Beni, and their team are accomplishing great exploits in changing people's lives—locally, nationally, and internationally. With his passion to know and please God, it is no surprise that Bethel Church has been effective and fruitful. This influence is marked by strong teaching and preaching accompanied by mighty signs and wonders—the result of cultivating a way of life that truly brings Heaven to earth.

Imagine if the church took this mandate seriously as Bill and his Bethel team have done? We will truly experience the greater works Jesus foretold we would walk in. We owe the world an encounter with God! This will not happen by remaining complacent, sitting around waiting for Jesus to return. The harvest is great, but the laborers are few. It is time to wake up, believe, and get to work.

I am very grateful Pastor Bill wrote this book. The words on these pages have the potential to ignite revival—not only in you, but the whole world. *The Way of Life* will awaken an insatiable desire within you to lay hold of Heaven's realities so that you can truly bring Heaven to earth.

—JOHN BEVERE
Minister and Cofounder of Messenger International
Bestselling author of *Good or God?; Killing Kryptonite; Driven by Eternity;* and *Drawing Near*

FOREWORD

by Katherine Ruonala

I remember when I first read Bill Johnson's book, *When Heaven Invades Earth*. I was so nourished by what I was reading that it took me three months to finish. Each paragraph was alive with revelation. It was revelation from a true apostolic teacher, backed up by testimonies, which stirred a fire in my soul, and there was a provocation on every page to pray and think deeply about what was being said. Reading through *The Way of Life* has been a similar experience for me as the Holy Spirit has prompted me numerous times throughout my reading to stop and respond to the wisdom that was being offered, and to consider how it needed to be applied in my life.

The invitation into applied wisdom is the gift we have been given in *The Way of Life*. As Bill so beautifully writes, wisdom that is not applied merely puffs us up, and so Bill has generously opened his heart and life to us to show us how he practically applies wisdom in his own life. For those who have ears to hear, this book is a precious treasure that gives us the privilege of sitting at a father's feet and hearing rich wisdom gained through a life of experience.

Over the years I have had the joy of ministering with quite a number of the leaders from Bethel Church, and one of the most wonderful things I have noticed is the way they all carry such a strong and consistent culture of open-hearted and genuine love and celebration of others. Jesus said, *"By this all will know that you are My disciples, if you have love for one another"* (John 13:35 NKJV). From the senior leadership of the church to the Bethel School of Ministry teams that are sent out worldwide, Bethel's core values are visibly demonstrated. *The Way of Life* brings insight into how Bill, a thought leader for a new generation of revivalists, and the team at Bethel have built this beautiful culture that is impacting the world.

In all our ways, God promises that if we acknowledge Him, He will make our paths straight (Proverbs 3:6), and the Holy Spirit wants to bring to our remembrance the words of Jesus. So my prayer for you as you enjoy reading this wonderful treasure is that you would be provoked as I have been to pray, "Holy Spirit, please help me to walk in applied wisdom today. Truly, Lord, show us Your paths and teach us *The Way of Life."*

—KATHERINE RUONALA
Senior Leader, Glory City Church, Brisbane, Australia
Founder and Facilitator of the Australian Prophetic Council, Senior
Leader of the Glory City Network, and host of Katherine Ruonala TV
Author of the bestselling books *Living in the Miraculous: How God's
Love Is Expressed through the Supernatural; Wilderness to Wonders:
Embracing the Power of Process;* and *Life with the Holy Spirit:
Enjoying Intimacy with the Spirit of God*

INTRODUCTION

My first international ministry trips, which began in 1986, were with a dear friend of mine, Dale Harrison. We have had such great times together, bringing the message of the Kingdom of God to several nations. A few years ago, Dale came to visit. We talked and caught up a bit on what was happening in our families and ministry life. Then he said something that stuck with me. He told me that I didn't realize how different the culture was at Bethel, but I needed to, and I needed to write about it in a book. I already had enough writing goals and assignments. I really didn't want to add to what was in my heart to write. But the main reason for my resistance to the idea was I didn't want to write about us. At all. Ever. But in all honesty, I couldn't shake it. I called him several weeks later and asked him to repeat his idea to me, as I felt *life* on what he said. He did, and I began to ponder the uniqueness of our world and took notes on what might be helpful to the broader body of Christ. *The Way of Life* is the result.

As much as I know how, I have avoided making this book about Bethel without robbing you, the reader, of the insights and experiences that have shaped our world.

For years, I have called Bethel "The Great Experiment." It really is, which means we succeed and fail. With that comes the privilege of learning what works and what doesn't. And that approach to life and ministry is an ongoing process, which implies we have not arrived to an elite status at all. We face that painful reality on a regular basis. And yet there is something happening here that I have ached for for so many years. I've learned it can be taught and imparted.

We have had breakthroughs that were once only dreams. We've also had levels of impact that were never even in our dreams. We have had extreme favor, and we've had tremendous opposition. Both of these realities were new to us. All of that is to say *we are in process.*

This book is my best attempt to speak of His great work of grace in us in a way that inspires unto hope, stirs up great faith, and releases an impartation for transformation. I offer this with the hope of seeing the full impact of the Gospel of the Kingdom on earth—in my lifetime. And if not mine, then in my children's lifetime.

I pray that from reading this, you will experience a breakthrough that will mark the rest of your life.

The passion of my heart is to represent God well, in all things. I long for His goodness, beauty, power, and dominion to be realized by everyone I know. The kingdoms of this world are becoming the Kingdom of our Lord and Christ. I hope that what is presented in this book will at least in part inspire a hunger for what might be possible in our lifetime—*"on earth as it is in heaven."*

Chapter One

THE GREATEST COMMISSION

When the dream of God becomes the most important part of our lives, a culture is formed that enhances our purpose for being. This is what brings us into our greatest possible delight.

The dream of God is to be discovered and embraced until it becomes our dream. And at least in part, that dream is that Heaven would come to earth. Sound impractical or impossible? Not to Him. It's in His heart, and it is well within His ability to complete, even through the finite efforts of those yielded to His purposes. It is our privilege to join in this endeavor by co-laboring with Him and watch Him add His wisdom and power to our prayers that we follow with simple obedience.

ASSIGNED BY GOD

The Bible frequently speaks of the responsibilities given to those who follow Jesus. But there is one assignment given that is so large, so all encompassing, that every other commission aligns its purpose to the fulfillment of that one. Perhaps we could call the other assignments *sub-points to one major point*. Each commission is vital and important because it serves the greater purpose. And the fulfillment is the realization of God's dream through the cooperation of those made in His image.

Our assignment as believers is a mandated focus that is to influence our relational journey with God. This becomes most evident in the discovery that our commission is to pray. And that prayer has a specific focus that is to become a vital part of our fellowship with God. Simply put, in the context of drawing near to our Father in worship and interaction, we are to lift up our voices, declaring, *"Your kingdom come, your will be done, on earth as it is in heaven"* (Matt. 6:10 NIV).

The assignments to evangelize, to work miracles, to care for the poor, the widow, the orphan, and the like are all practical expressions of this one major task—God's will fully manifest here, with Heaven as its source, model, and inspiration.

This task is not possible if we only discover the principles of God and follow them. Heaven itself thrives on the presence of God. Our commission is only possible with the increase of the overwhelming atmosphere of the glory of God that increases as we pray our assignment with faith. Those prayers must be followed with the risks necessary to display His will on earth. If there is any confusion on what that will looks like, look at how Jesus displayed the heart of His Father in His interaction with people in need, namely by eradicating disease, torment, and sin. Jesus Christ is perfect theology. And it is our privilege to illustrate the same reality that Jesus carried. Jesus declared it so when He said, *"As the Father sent me, I send you"* (John 20:21 MSG).

The reality of His world is so great that its effects must be anticipated in a way that can be measured. Our perception of unseen realities is powerfully influenced when we experience His presence.

For this reason, He says, *"Taste and see that the Lord is good"* (Ps. 34:8). What and how we see will always be influenced by what we experience.

We cannot allow ourselves to live in theory only. We do this whenever we embrace a routine of prayer without expecting an impact on the here and now. It is not wrong to look for evidence that our prayers are answered. If we become accustomed to praying prayers that aren't answered, we tend to settle for living in the realm of theory. Many resort to pretending they are being effective in their prayer assignment, looking only to eternity to measure success. Heaven/eternity is far greater than our wildest dream. But because of that greatness, we tend to hide our unbelief there, without any expectation for breakthrough here in the present. Whenever we do this, we rob ourselves of the personal strength and joy that was intended to be our possession as the result of answers to prayer. Answered prayer is God's design. We suffer in the long run when we expect our prayer assignment to be fulfilled in Heaven only.

THE ORIGINAL COMMISSION[1]

I love to study the commissions of God in the Scriptures. They all add something to the overall theme of the divine purpose for mankind. But it is the original commission that has really left a mark on my thinking and therefore on my approach to all the others.

> *God blessed them; and God said to them, "Be fruitful and multiply, and fill the earth, and subdue it"* (Genesis 1:28).

Be fruitful: lead a productive life where the fruitfulness of our labors helps to contribute to the overall wellbeing of what God has made.

Multiply: have children, who have children, who have children, all living under the beauty of His rule, illustrating the wonder of a perfect Father.

Fill the earth: spread throughout the world, bringing the influence of His Lordship through your lifestyle and service.

Subdue it: this implies there was already darkness and chaos outside of the Garden of Eden. *Subdue* is a military term that means to conquer. This was to be done by Adam and Eve, and their descendants, until the boundaries of the Garden of Eden covered the whole planet, placing it under the influence of God's perfect rule through His delegated ones.

In the Disciples' Prayer we find that God still longs for His world to influence and shape this one. Combining the *"on earth as it is in heaven"* (Matt. 6:10) with "go into all the world" (see Matt. 28:19), we see that His heart has not changed regarding our assignment. In many ways, when Jesus was resurrected He brought the keys of authority that man abandoned when we obeyed the serpent rather than God. When Jesus announced that all authority was now His, He was basically saying, "Now let's get back to plan A!"

THE OVERLAP

There are several commissions given to the 12 disciples during the time Jesus walked the earth. Toward the beginning of Jesus' ministry, they were commanded to *"heal the sick, raise the dead, cleanse the lepers, cast out demons"* (Matt. 10:8). And after Jesus was raised from the dead, they were told:

> Go therefore and make disciples of all the nations, baptizing them in the name of the Father and the Son and the Holy Spirit, **teaching them to observe all that I commanded you**; and lo, I am with you always, even to the end of the age (Matthew 28:19-20).

We could go on, but these two will work to illustrate my point. In spite of the uniqueness of their personalities, gifts, and calls, they were all given the same commission. To me that implies that the same assignment can be done differently, yet still be pleasing to the Lord. And while there are those who insist that certain parts of God's assignment for the 12 disciples are no longer valid, i.e. spiritual gifts, it is clear that Jesus intended for these responsibilities to continue throughout the age of the Church. He told the disciples to teach their converts to do *all* that Jesus taught them. That must include healing the sick as well as the other assignments given in Matthew 10 and Luke 9. It is not hard to see that Jesus intended for each generation of believers to embrace the responsibility to teach the following generation to do all that Jesus taught them to do. Changing that assignment and standard was never to take place. But it did.

LIKE CUTTING WOOD[2]

A number of years ago, I heard a pastor talk about a building project he once had to build a new sanctuary. He had such excitement for the new project, as this was to be a fulfillment of a vision for his growing church. We know that buildings are not the church; people are. Yet they can be wonderful tools that we use to facilitate the work of the ministry that ultimately impacts cities and nations.

He told us of how much he wanted to help in the actual building although he had no building skills. The contractor could see his excitement for the new project but also knew that he had no training in the skills needed for the job.

The pastor was persistent in asking if there was any work he could do. His enthusiasm over their building project finally persuaded the contractor to find something for him to do. While I admit I forgot the actual number, it was something like the following: He told the pastor that he needed 100 two-by-fours cut to eight feet in length for the next morning. This would be a great help as they would be able to get to work immediately upon arriving at the building site. The pastor was excited that he got to be involved in his own church project. So after everyone else left for the night, the pastor stayed and cut the lumber. He took the first piece of wood, measured eight feet with his tape measure, and marked it. He then carefully cut it to eight feet, exactly. Instead of using the tape to measure and cut the second piece of wood, he used the previously cut board, as he thought that would be much more efficient. He laid it on top of the uncut board, carefully drew a line where that board needed to be cut, and sawed off the part that was too long. He then took that newly cut board and placed it on top of the next piece that needed to be cut. He used this method of measuring throughout his assignment to cut 100 boards.

I'm sure you can see the problem. By using the previously cut board as the measure, the next board is marked and cut about one-eighth inch longer than the previous one. This process wouldn't have been so bad had he only had two or three boards to cut. But when that method is used for 100 boards, you end up with the ones at the end of the pile over nine feet long.

For 2,000 years, we've been comparing ourselves to the previous generation, noticing only slight differences. These "one-eighth-inch changes" seem rather harmless in the moment. But in the end, we end up with something that looks little like the example Jesus gave us in the beginning. And to protect our unbelief concerning our assignment—the great commission to disciple nations, displaying the greater works—many have found the need to create watered-down doctrines that dismantle the example and commandments that Jesus gave us.

It's crazy, but these people take it a step further by vilifying those who give themselves to rediscover the full intention of the commission that Jesus gave us all. It still amazes me to see how many fall for this deception. Instead of comparing ourselves with ourselves, we should have been using the original standard found in the life of Jesus so that the measure of God's goodness revealed in Christ, demonstrated in purity and power, would have remained the same through the past 2,000 years. Perhaps then we can see why He intended for us to do *greater works* than He did! (See John 14:12.) We would be building upon His example for centuries with fresh courage and great faith to see what might be possible in our lifetimes. Jesus only had three and a half years to discover what the Father would do through Him. We can learn this renewed standard by following His lead through the Holy Spirit and then building upon it to be able to complete the assignment given.

Our heavenly Father is truly bringing us back to the original measurement that He might be revealed more accurately as the Father who loves well.

CELEBRATING DIVERSITY

Every follower of Jesus is unique. Our gifts, personalities, backgrounds, and cultures all work to create a beautiful mosaic called the Church, the Body of Christ. It is interesting to note that unity is the result of the Holy Spirit's work in our lives. In fact, it is called, *"the unity of the Spirit"* in Ephesians 4:3. It's His. We are called to *"preserve"* this unity, not create it. It already exists wherever He has influence. And if it's not present, we've left His influence out of the equation. Second, it is of upmost importance to recognize that His kind of unity requires diversity. This is where individuals are valued for, and in spite of, their uniqueness. There is beauty in contrast.

This concept of unity through diversity is in opposition to the spirit of the day. There is strong political effort to erase the distinction of nations and people groups. Some call it globalization. Efforts have increased yet again to say there's no difference between humanity and animals. The absence of a creator/designer removes the possibility of a design, which exalts the opinions of the ignorant to divine status. That same spirit is now working to erase the distinction between male and female. This effort of the enemy of our souls is to blur what God designed and has called good. God's design is distinct and truly beautiful.

It is correct to say that individuality has merit, as God has no grandchildren. Each one must come before Him as an individual. But it is also true that there is a sameness that is equally important. We are all summoned by the Father to become like Jesus. It's the same call.

How wonderful that the life of Jesus, so perfect and complete, is able to flow through different personalities, giving unique flavors to what others are able to taste and see. The four Gospels illustrate this point quite well. The perspectives, values, callings of each writer are seen as they illustrate what it is to follow Jesus and become like Him. For example, Luke the physician shows a compassion and care that isn't as pronounced in Mark. The efficiency and economy of Mark's Gospel illustrates the most bang for your buck in this life as a disciple. As such, it is often referred to as the *businessman's Gospel.* You don't find that valuable trait in Luke. Similar things could be said of each of the four Gospels, not to mention the great diversity in the writers of the epistles. God seems to love and celebrate this theme.

Each of the writers in the New Testament reveals his individuality in what he wrote. Their personalities are visible without contaminating or distorting their revelation of Jesus. I find this to be so encouraging. I tend to become the weakest in faith when I compare myself to those whose gifts are so much different from mine, excelling in ways that I'll never be able to touch. Comparison is dangerous, and, in fact, it's deadly.

The call of God for each believer is equally diverse. The gifts and responsibilities are vast—so vast, in fact, that it will take the entire Church working together to accomplish the assignment given to us to re-present Jesus unto the discipling of nations.

PRAYER IS ASSIGNMENT ONE

As mentioned in the beginning of the chapter, we are to pray for His will to be done here just like in Heaven. That prayer assignment wasn't for eternity. It is for now.

Our God assignment reveals our reason for being alive. It is found in what is commonly called the Lord's Prayer. (That is not a good title for it, as in it is the confession of sin. Jesus, the eternal Son of God, had no sin. So I'll refer to it as the Disciples' Prayer.) The prayer goes like this:

> *Our Father who is in heaven,*
> *Hallowed be Your name.*
> *Your kingdom come.*
> *Your will be done,*
> *On earth as it is in heaven.*
> *Give us this day our daily bread.*
> *And forgive us our debts, as we also have forgiven*
> *our debtors.*
> *And do not lead us into temptation, but deliver*
> *us from evil. [For Yours is the kingdom and the*
> *power and the glory forever. Amen]*
> (Matthew 6:9-13).

Breaking it down in the following way will help to reveal the nature of our assignment.

Cultural Identity

"Our Father who is in heaven." Calling Him our Father is an affirmation of our identity as a family of sons and daughters and His place in our lives as the Almighty One.

Worship

"Father...Hallowed be Your name." Father is a holy and revered name of God. This is the key revelation Jesus brought to earth.

The Commissioned Prayer

"Your kingdom come. Your will be done, on earth as it is in heaven." This is our co-laboring assignment to reveal His heart to the nations.

Specific Application of the Commissioned Prayer

"Give us this day our daily bread. And forgive us our debts, as we also have forgiven our debtors. And do not lead us into temptation, but deliver us from evil." Answers to these requests are specific manifestations of the overall mandated prayer—*"on earth as it is in heaven."* The fulfillment of each is a practical manifestation of the answer.

Worship

"For yours is the kingdom and the power and the glory forever. Amen."

This prayer is an apostolic prayer. *Apostle* is a term used by both Greek and Roman armies to describe the leader of an entourage with the assignment to bring the culture of the conquering country to the one newly conquered. The purpose for this is fascinating. It was so that their ruler would feel as at home there as he did in his home country. Thus, we have, *"as it is in heaven."*

Our prayer assignment reveals God's overall commission and purpose for our lives. Through prayer, *"on earth as it is in heaven"* is to become an increasing reality. The Disciples' Prayer is an apostolic prayer in that it results in both miracles and transformation.

It's important to remember that He would never give us a prayer to pray that He didn't intend to answer. He's not a cruel taskmaster, giving us ritual and routine just to keep us busy. He is a Father. The creator God, the source of all design, is giving us direction and commands that are consistent with His divine strategy and purposes. He is the master builder, building for His intended outcome. And we get to play a part.

Because of the monumental size of the answer to this prayer, the temptation is to think this prayer is to prepare us for going to Heaven, or perhaps for the millennium. Historically, the Church tends to take

the greatest promises of Scripture and put them off into a period of time for which we have no responsibility. Jesus commanded His followers to do things that they might have impact now. His assignment to His followers was always to bring transformation to their immediate surroundings. In this prayer, we see the passion of the Father revealed as He invites us into interaction, which is a co-laboring partnership. It is here that we see the outcome as the invasion of His world into ours.

Three things need to be noted about this greatest of all commissions that we might be fully prepared for what God intends to do. The first is that God wants His world, Heaven, to have overriding influence on this one. In a practical sense, we must discover what that looks like. The second is that the process for this breakthrough is prayer. Prayer followed by action is exponentially powerful. What are the actions that should follow this kind of prayer? They are the specific commands listed in the other commissions—heal the sick, evangelize the world, disciple nations, etc. The act of prayer sets the stage for victory much like walking around the walls of Jericho set the stage for the walls to fall. Their collapse made it possible for Israel to go into the city and destroy their enemy. Prayer removes the obstacle (the wall) to our victory so that our actions help facilitate the fulfillment of what was prayed for (the Kingdom to come). In the assignment to pray, we have an invitation to come into His presence with confidence and co-labor with Him to see His purposes realized and established on the earth.

Third, we are to pray His heart, His dream. The Bible is filled with such insights into what His dream looks like. One of the expressions of this dream is to see the earth filled with His glory. Picture this, and never let it go—*the earth filled with the manifested presence of Jesus!*

Is this an impossible dream? Yes, if it's attempted in the strength and wisdom of man. But it's God's heart, revealed in Scripture. This is God's dream. So how is this going to happen? He will bring it to pass as we co-laborer with Christ. We have the privilege of establishing a culture that attracts Heaven. In my pursuit of *"on earth as it is in heaven,"* I've embraced certain values that have become part of the culture in both our personal and church life. The aspects of the culture we are experiencing in this move of God will be addressed in each chapter of this book.

Chapter Two

MEASURING HEAVEN

As mentioned earlier, when the surpassing greatness of His world touches this one, there must be ways to measure its effects. By design, Heaven is to influence earth. While we will never see nor understand all of the impact our life of faith has on the world around us, we can see some of it clearly. And we must.

We know that the devil came to kill, steal, and destroy. It is reasonable to conclude that the effects of his influence are measured by death, loss, and destruction. Jesus came to give life (see John 10:10). And in doing so, He came to destroy the works of the evil one (see 1 John 3:8). We must guard our hearts from the deception that attributes death, loss, and destruction to God. Our assignment becomes horribly weakened when we see God as the author of these things, as it is impossible to successfully believe for freedom when it is against our concept of the will of God. Freedom will only be experienced in the measure to which we see God as being good.

Jesus rebuked a storm. If that storm was the will of God the Father, then Jesus is fighting the will of God. The result is we end up with a divided house. We know that is not true as Jesus came to give life. Life shows up best where death once reigned.

Jesus measured the effects of Heaven and in turn taught us how to do the same. In Matthew 12:28, He said, *"But if I cast out demons by the Spirit of God, surely the kingdom of God has come upon you"* (NKJV). In this illustration, the enemy was involved in someone's life to kill, steal, and destroy. Jesus drove the demons out by the Holy Spirit, giving the person in need an encounter with God. That encounter brought the liberty that can only come as the result of His influencing presence. It's a beautiful picture of light driving out darkness. The Spirit of God comes upon a person to illustrate the Lordship of Jesus. Freedom is the result.

What then is the measurement of Heaven in this story? It is both in the absence of demons and the presence of freedom. The person being ministered to will have no difficulty in measuring the impact of Jesus' ministry. Those who were close to him or her will also have little challenge. Only the religious critics will debate this issue, as they have little ability to recognize the reality of the King and His Kingdom. The Pharisees in Jesus' day could watch a withered hand be healed and complain about the day the healing happened. When people lack the hunger for more of God and His full, present effect on humanity, they often become unable to recognize the presence of the Kingdom in what is displayed right in front of them. But for any honest seeker, freedom is easily recognized and celebrated, becoming the measurable effect of Heaven itself.

Creating a culture that measures impact is vital. The measurement is not to give us a personal grade of success or failure but to help us see whether or not our beliefs are supported by His manifested presence. This must be done that we might celebrate the power of the Gospel and give Him all the glory! This also provides me a moment of reality where I often see my need for more of Him to be manifest now. I must protect myself from the guilt or shame when there seems to be lack and turn my heart to seek His face even more. The presence of miracles in our lives is never to be used as a measuring stick to critique what might be deficient in another. We become no better than the Pharisees if that is our practice.

The effects of Heaven on earth are practical, gradual, and increasing wherever faith is exercised. Jesus often performed a miracle and then announced that His Kingdom was present or near. In other words, it was seen in the simple manifestation that brought an end to the devil's work of death, loss, and destruction, followed by the abundant life that only Jesus can give. The sickness or torment that was an evidence of the works of darkness was changed into a testimony of the fulfillment of His prayer—*"on earth as it is in heaven."* Simply put, there is no sickness there, so there is to be none here. There is no torment or sin in Heaven, so there is to be none here. We should never again question what God's will is in a given situation, if in fact it involves sin, sickness, or torment. It may be challenging. But it's not complicated.

His world is manifest in many ways, but there are three that are vital to the purpose of this book—power, purity, and culture. And of course, all of these exist because of, and are immersed in, love.

POWER

Over powers of darkness: The power of the Holy Spirit is perfectly suited for every true believer. We were created to carry and live in this power that the works of darkness would be destroyed. When we examine the life of Jesus, one thing becomes clear: He met every dark situation of lack, sin, torment, and disease with a redemptive solution. That is astounding! He never made an excuse for the problem. Nor did He allow the problem to remain. He always settled the issue by demonstrating what the Father's will looked like. What is equally important to see is that even when there was weak faith, He brought a miracle. Miracles testify of God's goodness. But they were also given as points of access to greater faith and increased awe and wonder of God Himself. Consider this: He never withheld the miracle because of weak faith. Christians will often tell someone they didn't get the miracle because their faith is small. That is tragic! Jesus never did that. What makes this even more appalling is that when people are hit with tragedy, the last thing they need is for a brother or sister in the Lord to get them to turn inward and examine their faith. Faith isn't found there. It's found in Christ. *"Fixing our eyes on Jesus, the author and perfecter of faith"* (Heb. 12:2).

Jesus would often address weak faith. But in every case, He followed His comment with a miracle, providing them access to greater faith. He addressed this in John 4:48: *"Unless you people see signs and wonders, you will by no means believe"* (NKJV)." Most of the time when I hear this taught, it is spoken of as a negative comment. They say it came out of His frustration over their unbelief in Him. First of all, that is not stated in the text but is taught that way because of our own issues of unbelief. Second, it is inconsistent with the rest of Jesus' teaching on the subject. John provides us with a sobering example. *"If I do not do the works of My Father, do not believe Me; but if I do, though you do not believe Me,* **believe the works, that you may know and believe** *that the Father is in Me, and I in Him"* (John 10:37-38 NKJV). This is astonishing. Without miracles (the works of the Father, see John 14:12), there is less access to the life of faith He desires of us. But when people see the touch of Heaven upon the earth, it is always redemptive but brings a requirement of a life change. Miracles are to bring us to repentance. Miracles then give us access to a measure of faith that is hard to develop otherwise. This is the testimony throughout the Gospels. People saw, and people believed.

Over personal flaws and weaknesses: It is vital that we see that His power in our lives is not just for how we minister to others. An interesting ministry standard was given in the Old Testament: *"You shall not muzzle an ox while it treads out the grain"* (Deut. 25:4 NKJV). That may seem like a strange verse for this subject, but think of it this way. A laborer for Christ must be able to eat from the product of their own labors. That means if I bring you freedom through the power of the Holy Spirit in my life, I must also learn to feed from the Holy Spirit that I might also live in complete freedom. Many come to Christ, get forgiven, but still carry the baggage of previous lifestyles into their walk with the Lord. Some come to Jesus for salvation but still have addictions to drugs, pornography, or things like gossip and slander. The point is, those things must change. And they change according to the work of the power of God in our lives. First Samuel 10:6 says that when the Spirit of the Lord came upon Saul, he turned into another man. The fact that he didn't maintain God's work in His life is not a testimony against the experience. It is the record of a man who did not steward the grace that God gave him for personal transformation. The bottom line is that when the Spirit of God came upon him, he was changed. He was free to become all God intended. The power of God is for personal freedom, that our character would be consistent with His power.

Endurance in difficulty: The hardest part of living in a miracle culture is waiting for the miracle. The battle is in the mind. And it can get pretty intense, especially when the miracle doesn't come quickly, or even at all. I have friends who have suffered greatly for the Gospel. They have been beaten, shot at, imprisoned, criticized, betrayed, and more. But before any of these happened at that level, they experienced an extremely powerful baptism in the Holy Spirit. They have said that without that encounter with God, they would have quit and lost heart. That baptism is for the purpose of power, miracle power. And sometimes that power is for the miracle of endurance.

Many tend to get introspective and self-condemning when there's a lack of breakthrough. This is such a big deal for us in our miracle culture that I wrote extensively about this in my book *Strengthening Yourself in the Lord*. But for now, let me just say, power is also needed for endurance. The manifestation of power upon the apostles was certainly for miracles. But perhaps what should stand out the most was their God-given ability to endure hardship without blaming God, themselves, or the people of God. This, in some ways might be the greater miracle. We must hold to the Word of God that says, *"All things work together for good"* (Rom. 8:28 NKJV). That promise wouldn't even be necessary for us if everything always worked the way we expected.

PURITY

Holiness is the beauty of God. The Bible says *"in the beauty of holiness"* (Ps. 96:9 NKJV). No one is more beautiful, more stunning, more attractive, more overwhelming in wonder, more glorious than Jesus. He is the person of holiness. And He is altogether lovely. In spite of this, most still don't have a proper understanding of righteousness or holiness.

The Church usually reduces this wonderful trait of God into a list of rules of what we can and cannot do. It's the beauty of God and His holiness that make that error so despicable. And yet I do understand the need for lists. Throughout history there have been those who confess Christ but live like the devil and call it grace. If our understanding of grace doesn't lead us to righteousness, we don't understand grace.

The reality of His world manifesting in my life is that I become more like Jesus. My responses to challenges, people, and the future are all to illustrate the impact of Heaven on earth. Jesus wants to be *re*-presented by every believer, so that the world will know what the Father is like. That is the simple but profound mandate. Reveal the Father. Reveal His glory, wonder, beauty, tenderness, compassion, and power. The list of possibilities is endless. When people see our lives and glorify the Father in Heaven, we have succeeded. Think of it this way—our lives enable them to draw near to God for themselves, giving Him the credit for what He has done in our lives. This positions them for their own relationship with Him and their own miracle of transformation.

> *Let your light shine before men in such a way that they may see your good works, and glorify your Father who is in heaven* (Matthew 5:16).

The effect of Heaven on earth is seen in my character. But it is also seen in my quickness to repent when I am wrong. That must include my readiness to clean up any mess I've caused. Sometimes we miss the chance to represent Him well in our conduct. We are then privileged to illustrate His goodness through our repentance.

Personal holiness is huge. But so is the corporate expression, which is seen in how we value and cherish other people. We have the privilege of celebrating others, treating them as Jesus treated His own. It is that holiness that defines us.

Here are just a few commandments given to us to fulfill this assignment:

> *With all humility and gentleness, with patience, showing tolerance for one another in love* (Ephesians 4:2).

> *Be kind to one another, tender-hearted, forgiving each other, just as God in Christ also has forgiven you* (Ephesians 4:32).

> *Be subject to one another in the fear of Christ* (Ephesians 5:21).

> *With humility of mind regard one another as more important than yourselves* (Philippians 2:3).

> *Therefore comfort one another* (1 Thessalonians 4:18).

> *Therefore encourage one another* (1 Thessalonians 5:11).

> *Live in peace with one another* (1 Thessalonians 5:13).

Seek after that which is good for one another and for all people (1 Thessalonians 5:15).

Let us consider how to stimulate one another to love and good deeds (Hebrews 10:24).

Do not speak against one another (James 4:11).

Do not complain, brethren, against one another (James 5:9).

Confess your sins to one another (James 5:16).

This is corporate holiness. The Bible is filled with such commands and assignments. They are not burdensome. They are opportunities to reveal what He is like to one another and to the world around us. It is the purity of Christ illustrated in how we value one another. In the same way that my natural body must care for all its parts, so the Body of Christ must do this to illustrate the continuity of His nature, which is holiness. There are many diseases in the world that are simply the body turning against itself. Crohn's disease is a great example, where the colon basically eats itself. As tragic as that is, it happens all the time in the church. To reject or turn against people is a disease of greater consequence than any physical disease.

CULTURE

Heaven to earth must go beyond our need for healing and deliverance. These things are necessary and are always expressions of the Father's love for us. But they are unto something. Fully realized, they are to have an effect on life as we know it.

Creating a culture in which the Gospel has an effect on all aspects of life is a most challenging part of our commission, as it has the greatest impact on the course of history. And yet, realized, this is where the beauty of God is found in the daily lives of civilization. I personally believe that this was the secret of the Reformation and the

Awakenings experienced in various nations around the world. His world has impact on *life as we know it*. Yet none of those times of refreshing from His presence carried all that He intended.

Culture is basically *the values, principles, beliefs, and attitudes that influence how life is lived in a specific location*. Every local church has a culture, as does every city and nation. The goal is to taste and see what it would be like to have Heaven's culture shape the value system of the world we live in. That may be hard for many to believe to actually happen in a nation. So at least start with your home or your local church. Let the small breakthroughs in culture be the prototype in your thinking for what God wants to do in the big picture.

Heaven's culture is first and foremost *presence-focused*. Everything in Heaven is connected to and thrives because of the presence of God. There is nothing in Heaven that exists apart from His presence. He is the beauty of that world. As worshipers, we are exposed to the surpassing greatness of His world. As a result, we are called to implement His *values* here.

It is safe to say that Heaven has a culture of honor. Under His Lordship, everyone is celebrated for who they are, without anyone stumbling over who they're not. Every feature of every life is a thing of beauty and value. The commands that God gives us about our relationships here only serve to mirror the reality that already exists in His world. It is possible to experience the lifestyle of Heaven now. Our manner of life can be shaped by the *lifestyles* of those in Heaven.

There it is. The measure of Heaven to earth is seen in the importance we place on His presence, His values, and His lifestyle. When the values of His world impact our daily lives, Heaven's culture becomes real and measurable.

OUR CULTURE OR KINGDOM CULTURE?

BUILDING A GREENHOUSE

The Netherlands is an amazing country known for many things, not the least of which are its dikes, windmills, wooden shoes, and tulips. And while that is obviously a rather touristy insight, it still has some merit. My friend and I were there to speak in a pastors' conference in the cold and damp month of November. We had a break one after-noon, and our host wanted to take us to see some of the sights his nation was known for. It was my first time in that country. I was excited to see some of the things I had only seen on postcards or on television. But because of the weather, we ended up driving past many of the typical destinations. It was just too cold and wet to get out of the car. Rather humorously, we looked out of the car window at the windmills and dikes as we drove past. At least we got to see them. But none of us wanted to get out of the car.

We soon arrived at the place he had in mind. It was a series of extremely large greenhouses where tulips were grown. From those greenhouses, their tulip industry sends flowers and bulbs all over the world. I have since read that the Netherlands provides somewhere around 85 percent of the world's supply of tulips.

When we entered the greenhouse, I was amazed at the color and the beauty of these flowers, seemingly beyond number. Row after row, section after section demonstrated their ability to grow beautiful flowers any time of year. While you'd never say it was warm inside, it was much more pleasant than it was outside. In fact, there was a bride in her beautiful bridal gown posing for her wedding photos next to one of the indoor ponds. Over the next hour or so of walking around all this beauty, we were deeply impressed by the splendor and excellence. It's impressive to me that someone figured out how to grow these flowers in the worst possible setting. The tulips that didn't have a chance to survive in the rather hostile weather outside thrived in the atmosphere provided by the greenhouse.

When the church discovers and lives in Heaven's culture while here on earth, we create an atmosphere that is very similar to the greenhouse in its effect over a city. In the right atmosphere (prevailing culture) we are more likely to grow the things we have vision for because the spiritual climate contributes to the vision and mandate of the Lord.

WHOSE CULTURE DO WE HAVE?

Because so many parts of the normal Christian culture are rarely challenged, we often make many assumptions on what is important and what is not. Most of us see through our own history, good or bad. It takes the renewing of the mind to see correctly.

I don't like the rebellious approach that implies everything is wrong and we need to question everything. But we often have "sacred cows" that we don't want anyone to touch. Those cows are our favorite imperfections that the Church sometimes wants to protect at all costs. Most of us have enough things in our thinking that need to change that I doubt we could handle it if God were to show us our need all at once. For me, it comes down to having absolute trust in Him in the journey. And that is a lot easier to do when I come completely abandoned and surrendered to His purposes, with no hidden agendas of my own. This really is the only way to come to the Lord of all—yielding to His Lordship.

CHURCH AS WE ALWAYS KNEW IT

All churches have a culture built into their existence. It's seen in their values; beliefs; expectations; relational boundaries; purpose; approach to money, success, people—both sinners and saints—and much more. It is our unwritten approach to life. Most of the time the culture that is built is not the actual culture of the Kingdom of God. In other words, it may be built to mimic the Christian principles that stand out to us yet not be the value system of Heaven itself. I know that sounds like a contradiction, but it isn't. It's extremely practical. Let me illustrate.

Most every ministry I know of takes this approach to finances: We know that each of us has a limited number of days on the earth. We also know that we have a limited amount of physical strength. Practically put, we know we can't skip sleep, food, or physical activity and have a long and healthy life. Ignoring those natural laws opens the door for the enemy of our souls to fulfill his self-appointed assignment *to kill, steal, and destroy* us. Our neglect of the natural gives him the legal right to have negative impact on the spiritual part of our lives. Now contrast that reality with this fact: We have access to unlimited resources. In the same way Jesus multiplied food or instructed the disciple to get the gold coin out of the fish's mouth, so we live with a God-given access to provision that has no end or limit. According to Scripture our provision of resources is *"according to His riches in glory"* (Phil. 4:19). If there was ever a statement that should overwhelm our hearts and minds, it would be this one. That standard for divine provision is an eternal, inexhaustible resource. Yet the normal ministry spends—to a point of exhaustion, abuse, and neglect—what is limited (time and strength) to save what is unlimited (resources). And then we call it good stewardship. That just might be the arm of the flesh attempting to create a biblical culture that does not exist in Heaven.

I offer another example to give a very small illustration of the difference between Heaven's culture and Christian culture. People who burn themselves out for the Gospel are heralded as heroes. Books are written about them. And then this problem is further developed in Church culture as we celebrate pastors who never take a day off. The Church celebrates them for their sacrificial love for the people in the church. If you've ever travelled by an airplane, you've heard the flight attendant tell the passengers, "If you need oxygen, a mask will fall from the ceiling. Put it on yourself first, then on those around you who need assistance." It is not love to choose those around you in this context, as you might not be around long enough for it to matter. We forget the fact that these pastors we've heralded as heroes had to violate a commandment of the Lord for rest. And when they often lose their families or their health, we blame that tragedy on the spiritual warfare that spiritual leaders face. I don't disagree that there was warfare. But our foolish decisions empower the powers of darkness. Our values are often twisted and have nothing to do with the Kingdom of God. The *"on earth as it is in heaven"* must take on literal application if we're to have the effect of *salt* on the world around us that God intended. I really don't mean to shame anyone. I've made my share of foolish attempts to honor God. We just need to wake up to the reality of Heaven, and how it will affect how we think and live, and turn completely to Him and His Word.

I write these things to bring hunger. How much of the prayer *"on earth as it is in heaven"* are we willing to pursue? Apparently, the fulfillment of this prayer is possible in our lifetime, or it wouldn't have been given to the disciples as the model prayer for now. Jesus is not known for giving His followers an exercise in futility. His commands are never to keep us busy. They are redemptive in nature, revealing His heart for people.

Jesus didn't put a limit on the amount of Heaven's influence on earth. Neither should we. When Jesus gives a direction in prayer, He is revealing His heart and His will for our lives. This is the process through which He intends to fulfill our purpose. He is showing us the prayer the Father longs to answer. It is important for us to realize the process God uses to fulfill His intent through our lives—prayer. What we take possession of in prayer we'll be able to more correctly steward in life. These battles are won on our knees before they are lived out on our feet.

The overall mandate of this kind of lifestyle is the continual hunger for more. It is the culture of the Kingdom of God, where we maintain joyful thankfulness, but also ever-increasing hunger for what might be possible in our lifetime. This is truly our mandated lifestyle.

FREEDOM TO EXPERIMENT

Establishing His will in the earth seems rather simple on paper, but in real life it requires a willingness to try, fail, and try again. I have learned little in this life of faith apart from the freedom to experiment. Rarely does a child ride a bike successfully on the first attempt. That's why I taught my kids to ride at the park where there was a lot of grass so that *when* they fell, they fell on the grass. As much as was possible, they fell safely, which I believe to be an often-forgotten responsibility of pastoral care. Many leaders think their job is to discourage people from trying, so then they won't fail. When I speak of failing, I'm not referring to moral or ethical failure or experimenting with lifestyles that are contrary to the teaching of Scripture. I am referring to the God-given desire to learn how to represent Jesus well in purity and power. We become most productive when our hunger for fulfilling His mandate for our lives is greater than our fear of failure. I believe the willingness to fail is a necessity for growth, especially as we hunger for the biblical realities that are no longer the norm for the New Testament Church. Someone has to get the breakthrough so the others can benefit.

I remember when I first started pastoring Bethel Church in Redding, California. On one of the first Sundays, I announced that my lifestyle required the liberty to experiment. My practice is to do so in relationship with people of like mind so together we stay accountable. I then announced that if the people in the church didn't like it when things didn't work well the first time around, I would make them very uncomfortable, and that they might want to consider attending one of the many other fine churches in our city. It wasn't as rude as it sounds in print. But it was honest. I believe this is my call in life. While wisdom and loving care for people must always be evident, supernatural breakthroughs are equally necessary for all of us to grow into God's dream for us. After all, He has destined me to be like His Son Jesus, in purity and power. The reality is someone else may get the breakthrough before I do. That's wonderful! It's not a race against other believers. It's a race against time. But often the absence of examples to follow in the supernatural parts of our faith is what makes experimenting an even greater part of our lives.

BREAKING BARRIERS

There once was a barrier in people's thinking regarding how fast a man could run. Even some doctors and scientists stated that it was physically impossible for a human being to run a mile faster than four minutes. They were able to substantiate their conclusions with scientific principles and facts. Their reasoning seemed to adequately explain why it had never been done before. But there were several individuals who didn't believe the conclusion of the so-called experts. One such person was Roger Banister, a medical student in the UK. On May 6, 1954, he ran one mile in 3 minutes and 59.4 seconds. The crowd went wild, and a huge barrier had been broken, both athletically and mentally. The record didn't last long. Several other runners broke his record in the weeks and months that followed. Banister got through a psychological barrier that seemed to benefit others. It really is similar to how breakthroughs happen in the Kingdom of God.

History shows wonderful outpourings of the Spirit that happen in one part of the world. And then without any communication or geographical connection, the same outpouring takes place in another part of the world, sometimes within days or weeks of the other. Of course, God's sovereign touch is always an explanation, which would be right and true. But we are not programed robots. It can also be said that when a follower of Jesus hungers beyond their fear of failure, breakthroughs happen. And when that breakthrough happens in one place, it opens the door for others to benefit with an outpouring of their own. The testimony of God's faithfulness creates a draft drawing others into the purposes of God, sometimes without much effort or fanfare.

The Church in our day is learning to let go of old mindsets, embrace a truly biblical worldview, and boldly enter into the promises of God in ways we never thought were possible. This is our privilege and our mandate.

Chapter Four

CORNERSTONES
OF THOUGHT

Many years ago, I ministered in a city known for the cult head-quarters established there. What impacted me greatly about this trip was the fact that so many people in the area were not a part of the cult, but had still lived under its influence. This group had developed a culture that influenced an entire region, although I doubt the residents were aware of what had been happening to them. Their "religious" culture sat like a blanket of fog over the region, influencing values and perception of what is to be expected from life.

On my flight home, I pondered what I had just witnessed—culture impacts everyone. Then it hit me—if this can work in the negative, then it should be able to work in the positive. My conclusion was that Kingdom-oriented people can influence their surroundings to the point that residents, including those who will not believe our message, will still live under the influence of the Kingdom of God displayed in a region. My assignment just became clearer. From that point on, I began to study culture, considering the many ways the Church can have influence on our cities.

APPLE UNIVERSITY

Through the years, I've read quite a few articles and books on Steve Jobs and Apple, which is in many ways the world's most successful company. This company has fascinated me since my first computer purchase in 1990. While it is neither my desire to promote their products nor to find things to criticize, I simply admire their success. Success is much more than the amount of money in their accounts. They have shaped the culture around them in part because they have a culture within the company that is unique. We would do well to learn from them.

Realizing that Apple was unlike any other company, Steve Jobs hired Joel Podolny, the then dean of Yale School of Management. His job was to study the culture of Apple. Jobs knew that his company was different. If they could identify "why and how" they were different, they could be more intentional in training new employees in their way of thinking. Thus, Apple University was created. Very little is known about this university, as secrecy remains a core value at Apple. But we know the basic concept is to train new employees.

This seemed brilliant to me, as we don't always know what we know. In our world, I often am guilty of assuming that people know something when they don't at all. It's one of the reasons I love doing question and answer times, as it is in those moments I start to realize more fully how much I assume people know.

Identifying what makes Apple tick enables them to reproduce more effectively and intentionally. I would love to see more churches and Kingdom-oriented ministries do the same—study their own culture to identify what works and what doesn't and why. Instead of assuming that our culture is truly Kingdom, examine it through the lens of Scripture, making whatever adjustments are necessary.

THE FOUR CORNERSTONES OF THOUGHT

This journey helped me to identify four cornerstones of thought that have helped shaped the culture in our world over the last 20-plus years. A single act does not create a culture. But when these values become instinctive reactions to problems or opportunities, they become culture.

God Is Good

I consider this to be the cornerstone of our theology. He is as good as He is holy. I don't know anyone in the faith who would disagree with this statement of God's goodness. If we're honest, we have to believe it, as it is in the Scriptures. It's not the statement of faith that needs adjusting as much as it is our definition of His goodness that needs attention. God is credited with many horrible things because of the thought He is God and in control of everything. It is true that God is in charge, but I wouldn't agree that He is in control. He is God and can force His purposes on all He has made, should He want to. But He has chosen to create something called free will, and in doing so made it possible for things to happen He didn't approve of. "[God is] *not willing that any should perish but that all should come to repentance*" (2 Pet. 3:9 NKJV). Is anyone perishing? Yes. Is it His will? No. So we can't afford to come to such careless conclusions, just because we haven't seen the breakthrough we've been praying for.

Every parent should understand the difference between *control* and *in charge*. We are in charge of our households, but not always in control of what happens there. God created a world in which our wills would have an effect on the outcome. And in turn we were written into His sovereign plan.

If I did to my children what many think God does to His, I'd be arrested for child abuse. What helps me most in this subject is looking to the life of Jesus. He is perfect theology. He perfectly illustrates the Father in every way. He never turned anyone away, regardless of the depth of his or her sin or whether he or she had great or little faith concerning their need.

Jesus rebuked a storm. If the Father sent the storm, then Jesus rebuked the Father's will, which we know didn't happen. That would be a divided house, which cannot stand. Instead Jesus rebuked the storm because something demonic was behind it. The storm opposed the purposes of the Father in the life of Jesus and His disciples.

He also never allowed a sickness to remain. In every case where there was a willingness to come to Jesus, they left His presence healed. He reveals what happens when God is in control, as the deficiencies of life are brought under His Lordship, His Kingship. When His Kingdom comes, disease and torment leave.

Nothing Is Impossible

Without this important point, we live intimidated and somewhat controlled by the evil circumstances of life. It becomes all too easy to accept things as they are, without carrying the responsibility to address these things in Jesus' name. An assumption is then made that whatever happens was meant to be.

We know that God alone lives in the realm where nothing is impossible. He is God. He is infinite, while everything else is finite. There is one beautiful exception to this rule—He made it possible for those who believe Him to experience the same reality He does. *"Nothing is impossible for those who believe"* (see Matt. 17:20). Faith gives us access to a realm known only to God. This is the privilege given to His children, to those who believe.

I'll never forget the first time it became obvious that people were living with this conviction. They got excited when they were told someone who was dying of cancer was attending a wedding. Three or four people came to me before the wedding started with a sense of joy for the opportunity to see that disease put in its place in Jesus' name. In each case, they thought that God had brought that person to be healed. Whenever we become people who truly believe that nothing is impossible with God, we look for problems. (By the way, this man was healed during a prayer time following the wedding.)

People often tell me that they know God can heal them. That's a great place to start. But it is a sobering fact that the devil himself has that much faith. He too knows God can heal a person. Faith is one of the ways that God releases His healing grace, so it might be good to find ways to strengthen our faith. Primarily that means we have to exercise the measure we've been given.

Jesus' Blood Paid for Everything

When Jesus hung on the cross, He made one final statement: *"It is finished"* (John 19:30). His job was completed. Everything that needed to be done for our eternal destiny was accomplished in that moment. The ramifications of this fact are far reaching. There is nothing that we will ever need, even 100 billion years from now, that will not have been provided for at the cross. It was that complete.

It can be said that it will take the ages to come just to scratch the surface of understanding the richness of His grace: *"so that in the ages to come He might show the surpassing riches of His grace in kindness toward us in Christ Jesus"* (Eph. 2:7). But it all points back to the cross of Jesus, that place of great suffering and death.

There is nothing that will come up at any time in the future that would require God to do something in addition to the redemptive work on the cross. It truly is finished.

Each Person Is Significant

It is easier to place the title of significance on an individual who has accomplished much. And that would be true, but not the whole truth. Every person is significant in God's eyes, and therefore must become so in ours.

There are times when I come upon a person who is behaving in an almost inhuman way, actually more like an animal. Only God knows what brought them to such a place of devastation. And while

I've protected myself from looking down at such individuals, it's a challenge to see their significance. I remind myself that when they were born, someone looked at that baby and commented how cute they were. It's not a mental game. It's a reminder that rarely are people born in such a place of disrepair. And if they are, they are still valuable to Jesus and must become valuable to me.

Sometimes we do better at recognizing the importance of another person, but struggle with our own value. This also is something that must change. We are so resistant to self-centeredness and pride that we often overreact and create habits of self-criticism and self-judgment in its place. We are to love others as we love ourselves. If we have little realization of our value in God's eyes, it will show in how we love others. We can't help but be faulty in that assignment.

I'm always careful with those who are very self-critical, as they will probably love me as they love themselves. The overemphasis on self, even if it's self-criticism, is still focused on self.

I remind you, again, that under the King's dominion every person is celebrated for who they are without anyone stumbling over who they are not. Sometimes I'll hear someone make a comment that goes something like this: "That person has a strong prophetic gift, but they couldn't administrate their way out of the room." What just happened? They acknowledged a gift, but not without a point of criticism. Is that necessary? Not really. Even if I have the responsibility to disciple that person, I will take a completely different approach to training them where they are weak. But the inability to celebrate a person without a criticism is a great weakness on our end.

When we know who He made us to be, we'll never want to be anyone else. He has wrapped up His significance in the destiny of every person He called to Himself for salvation.

One of the most important parts of recognizing a person's significance is that Jesus chooses people long before they could earn such favor. One of my favorite portions of Scripture in this regard is found in Isaiah 61. This is the passage that Jesus quotes when He starts His ministry in Luke 4. This is where the Spirit of the Lord comes upon Him for healing, deliverance, and restoration of broken lives. It is such a beautiful passage. But it takes us to a profound conclusion:

> Then **they** will rebuild the ancient ruins,
> **They** will raise up the former devastations;
> And **they** will repair the ruined cities,
> The desolations of many generations (Isaiah 61:4).

Who are "they"? It's the afflicted, brokenhearted, captives, prisoners, mourners, burned-out ones, and the fainting ones because of weakness described in verses 1-3. Think about this. The most broken in society, the ones the Church often rejects, and society certainly rejects, are the ones anointed by God to rebuild our cities that have been destroyed through devastation. They are the builders. Seeing their significance before they have earned it is actually what positions them for their own breakthroughs in ways that are valuable to entire cities. How we treat these disenfranchised, considering their significance in God's eyes, becomes key in seeing our cities restored to God's design and purpose.

BEHAVIORS PROVE BELIEFS

The four cornerstones of thought in our biblical worldview are these: *God is good, nothing is impossible, the blood of Jesus paid for everything,* and *every person is significant.* When these life-changing truths are truly embraced, they shape how we think and what we value. But how do we know when they have truly become a part of us? That really can only be done when our behavior illustrates what we really believe. Each of these four cornerstones of thought has specific behaviors that prove how deeply the truth has impacted our lives. And we all have room for improvement.

It is very easy to say "amen" to any of these truths when we hear it spoken. When someone says, "God is good," the response is often, "all the time." That is so true, but is it what I really believe? What I really believe is seen in my lifestyle. Behavior begins as an action, but matures into a reaction. In other words, what is my first response when I face a problem or even an opportunity? If it's fear or anxiety, that's not a time for shame or guilt. It's a time to surrender our hearts to the only One who gives us the grace to respond like Him. Our reactions reveal our internal culture. And if you're like me, my reactions are more Christ-like today than they were 20 years ago, but I still have a way to go before I can honestly say, "I *only* do what I see my Father do. I *only* say what I hear my Father say."

GOD IS GOOD—DREAM BIG!

If I truly believe that God is good, it will be seen in my ability to dream big. And I don't mean our night dreams, although there are times when those are included in this equation. We have an obligation to the Lord and to the world around us to dream God-sized dreams that only He can fulfill. There's something about His nature as a Father that can only be realized through the fulfillment of the dreams of His people. His heart is then revealed for all to see. I believe there will be a generation who will dream dreams that God is totally devoted to. And as they glorify Him, the redemptive work of Jesus will become famous.

It was in the context of friendship with God (see John 15:15) that Jesus stated four times in three chapters that we could ask for whatever we wanted and it would be done for us. (See John 14:13; 15:7,16; 16:23-24.) In light of that, I remind you that He always reserves the right to say no to any prayer that undermines our purpose. We know that God did not invite us to become self-centered Christians who demand our own way before the Almighty God. This isn't an invitation into selfishness. Instead, it's an invitation to co-labor with the Lord, once again through prayer. And while it is accurate to say He's not inviting us to increase our self-centeredness, neither is He making us robots where He programs us to pray certain things so He can answer them. He invites us into a relationship where our desires move Him. The Almighty God makes Himself vulnerable to the desires of His people. I sometimes wonder how much of what we're seeing in the earth, or perhaps even what we're not seeing, is the direct result of His children's dreams or the lack thereof.

Our faith only explores where we know God is good. It's as though our understanding of His goodness is an invitation to explore that territory through faith. This is our reality. And if I believe He is as good as He is holy, then I have no excuse not to dream big. It's required of me. I cannot coast through life when I see His nature is as wonderful as it is. I must learn to respond to it with permission, to represent His heart in the earth through my creative capacity to dream.

NOTHING IS IMPOSSIBLE—TAKE RISKS

When I truly believe nothing is impossible for God *and* nothing is impossible for those who believe, I will respond to that inward conviction of the heart by recognizing I carry solutions for the death, loss, and destruction that plagues humanity. When I find them, I must take the risks necessary to see the situation changed for the glory of God. Jesus both lived and died that this might become our reality. This is the normal Christian life.

John Wimber used to say, "Faith is spelled R-I-S-K." It's true. That basically means we work to create a time and place for the Extravagant One to show up and do what only He can do. We make the room, whether it's in a church meeting or whether it's in our friendship with a neighbor. We make the room for God to come and do as He pleases through our obedience to His will—*"as it is in heaven."*

If I have no cash on hand nor any way to get it and a person in need asks for money to buy a meal, I can honestly say, "I'm so sorry, but I don't have it to give." But if I have hundreds of dollars in my wallet and a person in need asks for money for a meal, I can't say I don't have it. In the second illustration, I am aware of what I have with me. Believers who live conscious of the Spirit of God in their lives and what He has come to do in and through them cannot say to the one in need, "I'm so sorry. But I don't have it to give." It says of Jesus, *"He healed all, for God was with Him"* (see Acts 10:38). If the Spirit of God is with us, He expects us to invade the impossible in His name. The Holy Spirit is the Spirit of the resurrected Christ. He raised Him from the dead. And it's that Holy Spirit who flows through us to alter the course of history for His name's sake.

JESUS' BLOOD PAID FOR EVERYTHING—I OWE HIM MY COMPLETE TRUST

Perhaps this is so obvious that some might think it's not worth mentioning. But I think it is. Because Jesus took care of everything at Calvary, I owe Him my trust when things do not look good or according to what I felt was promised to me. Our lives are comprised of acts of faith, as well as an abiding trust. Recent experiences helped me to see that bold faith stands on the shoulders of quiet trust. This is developed in our lives when things look different from what we had planned or prayed for. Nurturing this kind of trust is so important to God and important for the development of Christ-like character in us. It's that vital to our life in Christ. It is one of the two absolutes for the life of the believer—love and faith. We know the *"greatest of these is love"* (1 Cor. 13:13) and *"without faith it is impossible to please Him"* (Heb. 11:6). In Galatians 5:6, the apostle Paul states that faith works through love, revealing that by God's design these are to work in tandem. Another way to put it is that these are two sides of the same coin.

My absolute trust in Him is because I truly believe that Jesus really did cover everything I'll ever need, for all eternity, when He

suffered in my place on the cross. Because it was complete, I owe Him my complete trust when things look different than expected.

> *He who did not spare His own Son, but delivered Him over for us all, how will He not also with Him freely give us all things?* (Romans 8:32)

This passage is one of the most convicting and freeing verses in the Bible for me. It really is the biblical basis for this statement—*I owe Him my complete trust.* If the Father offered His own Son for our salvation, everything else is included in that extreme gift. Nothing else we will ever need will be able to compete in significance with that one gift. Because of this fact, it becomes rather foolish to question His heart in caring for the other needs in our lives.

WE ARE SIGNIFICANT—SERVE WELL

One of the main focuses of our ministry is to help people in their identity in Christ. So few people have what we'd call a healthy self-esteem in their place before the Father as a son or daughter. So many good people have fallen into this trap of unbelief about their own identity in Him. Tragically, this habit is thought by many to be humility. And any time we give a virtuous name to a defect, we give it permission to stay and gain influence. It isn't humility. It usually reveals our own unbelief.

As people begin to grow in their understanding of their identity in Christ, the growth often comes in phases, just as when we were children. One of the most constant mistakes is when people grow in their identity through a title or how they function in a spiritual gift. I am not my gift or title. I am a child of God. Period. Whenever we build our identity around our title, we turn to a performance mentality in serving the Lord. It's just not healthy. Our own emotional, mental, and spiritual stability become compromised with this posture. We are stable only when we see ourselves as a child of God.

One of the most significant moments in Jesus' life is found in John 13. This is where Jesus washed the disciples' feet. This was a commissioning of sorts as He set the direction for their thinking and values from that point on.

> *Jesus, knowing that the Father had given all things into His hands, and that He had come forth from God and was going back to God, got up from supper, and laid aside His garments; and taking a towel, He girded Himself. Then He poured water into the basin, and began to wash the disciples' feet and to wipe them with the towel with which He was girded* (John 13:3-5).

These verses are fascinating because they talk openly about what Jesus had on His mind. First of all, He was aware that the Father had given everything into His hands. The eternal Son of God surrendered everything to become a man and now re-inherited everything as the Son of Man. This is a stunning picture of the sacrifice that was made for us. He did this so we could be included in an inheritance. Second, He knew He came from the Father and was now about to return to Him. It was in that context, with an awareness of extreme personal significance, that He rose from supper, girded himself with a towel, and washed His disciples' feet.

In our environment, I know when a person truly sees their significance, as no position of service is too low. Serving well tarnishes neither their self-esteem nor their need for respect from others. Jesus is the ultimate model of this as He uses this moment to honor those who would now carry His name into the earth, and He commissions them to do the same. Serving well is how we respond to really seeing our significance.

CREATING CONTEXT

These four cornerstones of thought help to create a culture in which the people of God succeed in purpose. These values serve to form an atmosphere where God's heart is discovered and demonstrated openly in the corporate gatherings, spilling over into the communities we love and serve. Carrying God's heart in this manner helps to create a context in which we display who He is and what He is like. He is the perfect Father.

Chapter Five

APPROACHING LIFE

What we think is possible during our lifetime has a radical effect on our approach to life. The believer has an advantage as we have the privilege of living with no impossibilities. If this becomes true in our attitude and thoughts, it helps to shape our worldview.

These preset values are much like the default on a computer. The word processing program on my MacBook Pro already has a font chosen, the size of that font, the page layout, etc. In life, we have similar preset values. They heavily influence our immediate reaction to a problem or an opportunity. When those values are more than concepts, but are the burning convictions based on what God says about life, they enable us to perceive more than would naturally be possible. But if those values are shaped by secular culture, our disappointments, or even certain parts of Church history, they influence our perspective dramatically away from God's purpose and plan. This is a huge issue, for if my approach to life is different from His, I will develop a culture around me that supports my view. These cultures sustain errors in thought, ambition, and faith. Here's an example: The mere expectation of evil increasing in the earth, without a conviction of

God's heart for answers, creates a people without hope. In a strange sense, we then become a people who are encouraged over the increase of evil, as it becomes a sign that we are in the last days spoken of in Scripture. We must never find encouragement in the lack of breakthrough of Kingdom realities. It is time to make a decision not to embrace any theology for the last days that doesn't require faith to see it happen.

Many believers answer my challenge by saying their hope is in the return of Christ. While His return is more glorious than any of us could possibly imagine, our faith must produce impact on the realities we face now. It is a weak Christian culture that allows and sometimes gives honor to those who have a faith in the return of Jesus but have little to no faith in the power of the Gospel to effect change right now. Once again, faith then becomes untested and unproven without a measurable impact on the world around us. Our expressions of faith must have an effect on the death, loss, and destruction we are confronted with on a daily basis. These tragic realities are the enemy's fingerprints. Our faith must be a *right now faith* that replaces the fingerprints of darkness with the fingerprints of a loving Father who sent His Son to redeem, restore, rebuild, and renew. This is faith touching the *now* of life.

THE BEAUTY OF WISDOM

Wisdom is often thought of as the more stoic part of life. It is often treated as the ability to solve problems or make difficult decisions. As important as that may be, this good but anemic definition has removed wisdom from its place of significance in much of church culture. According to Scripture, wisdom is the principal thing and is to be sought after as a priority.

> *For wisdom is better than jewels; and all desirable things cannot compare with her* (Proverbs 8:11).

If wisdom is to have such a primary place in our lives, then a culture of wisdom is to be expected, impacting the world now.

Many things around us are good, important, and desirable. Yet *"all desirable things cannot compare to wisdom."* Nothing we could desire is better than or *equal* to the value of wisdom. Interestingly, pursuing wisdom is prioritized much like *"seeking first the Kingdom of God"* is in the New Testament. Throughout Proverbs, seeking wisdom is what releases the blessing of God in all the other areas of life. Whether health, finances, position and title, or the beauty of meaningful relationships, all are enhanced and enabled through our prioritized pursuit of wisdom. This journey brings us to the wonderful discovery that wisdom is also a person. Jesus is our wisdom (see 1 Cor. 1:30).

Wisdom is a person, so living in wisdom is a relationship where we learn to truly see through His eyes, gaining His perspective. And it is that perspective that enables faith. It could be said that wisdom gives faith a context in which to function. In the same way that the banks of a river give direction to the water, so wisdom gives faith a direction, a target.

WISDOM AND PRAYER

One of the most interesting aspects of wisdom is that it reveals the nature of God in a way similar to prayer. Because of this, wisdom is uniquely connected to our prayer lives. By nature, it reveals God as a covenant-making Father, who longs to answer the cries of our hearts. Proverbs 8:34 says, *"Blessed is the man who listens to me, watching daily at my gates, waiting at my doorposts."* Now compare this with Jesus' command in Matthew 7:7 concerning prayer: *"Ask, and it will be given to you; seek, and you will find; knock, and it will be opened to you."* Jesus said to **ask**, and wisdom says *"blessed is the man who **listens** to me."* Jesus said to **seek**, and wisdom says to *"**watch** daily at His gates."* Jesus said to **knock**, and wisdom says to *"**wait** at His *doorposts.*" The divine partnership illustrated in the beauty of the covenant of prayer is actually made possible through the expression of wisdom.

WISDOM'S EXPRESSIONS

There are many wonderful ways to accurately define and demonstrate wisdom. But my present focus is the three expressions of wisdom that enable us to shape culture. Those three are creativity, excellence, and integrity.

CREATIVITY

Wisdom itself was with God on the day of creation, as it is by nature an influence through creative expression. Proverbs chapter 8 helps us to see wisdom's role in creation in a way that could otherwise be forgotten. Several facts stand out to me in this chapter:

- Wisdom is the architect of creation (vs. 30).

- Wisdom is the Father's delight (vs. 30).

- Wisdom rejoices before the Father (vs. 30).

- Wisdom rejoices (celebrates with laughter) over the inhabited world (vs. 31).

- Wisdom delights in humanity (vs. 31).

- Wisdom in us increases our favor with God (vs. 35).

From these passages, we see that wisdom is anything but stoic. Wisdom captures and expresses the emotion and intellect of Heaven itself. The Father celebrates wisdom. It celebrates the wonder of creation with laughter. It expresses great joy. It builds with pleasure and loves people. Wisdom seems to model excitement for life itself, for it always anticipates the heart of God being manifest in any given situation. Wisdom always perceives God's purpose and design and works to demonstrate it clearly. As a people who are in pursuit of wisdom we must learn to manifest these traits in our approach to life, successfully bearing the fruit of wisdom.

As wisdom is the architect of creation, it must inspire a creative expression in those who seek her. In other words, wisdom enables us to be creative. I grew up in an artist's home. Our home was filled with music, beautiful paintings, and great design. While we were never wealthy, our home was often more beautiful than those of our wealthy friends. The reason was that wisdom was demonstrated through creative expression through both my mom and dad. Having said this, it would be a mistake to think that creativity is only seen in what is typically called art—painting, singing, acting, etc. Everyone in Christ—the doctor, the accountant, the schoolteacher, the lawyer, the stay-at-home mom, etc.—is able to express wisdom through creativity. This is where wisdom becomes manifest in a way that impacts the world around us the most—by wisdom touching the mundane.

The Queen

The Queen of Sheba came to Solomon with all kinds of questions. He answered each one with such depth, and she was overwhelmed by his wisdom. But none of her questions were listed in Scripture. I would have loved to hear those questions and his answers. This is a very notable moment where God is silent. Sometimes His silence shouts a message we couldn't otherwise hear. If He had mentioned them, we probably would have missed the most significant part of the story—while his answers impacted her significantly, it was the mundane things, touched by wisdom, through which God chose to display the place of wisdom in day-to-day life. Clothes, plates, stairs, and the like were the things listed that convinced her of Solomon's wisdom and ultimately of the God of Israel (see 1 Kings 10:1-7).

Nothing could be more mundane than plates, clothes, and stairs, yet those were the things that made God's list. This tells me that some of the more boring parts of life, the parts that we often take for granted, are crying out to be touched by wisdom. Once touched by God's wisdom, they are moved from the boring to the significant, from the mundane to the things that reveal the actual nature of God![3]

Creativity as a Cultural Value

Dreams often become aborted because of the absence of creative expression in a culture. Wherever creative thinking is missing, God-given dreams are thought to be impractical and undoable. When creativity becomes the norm, people tend not to respond to challenges with, "Oh, that's not a possibility." Creativity says we'll find out how to do it. Wisdom lives from the place of faith that believes *"with God all things all possible"* (Matt. 19:26).

I intentionally surround myself with people who think creatively. I don't want to consult with people who don't look for solutions. Few things are more frustrating than presenting an idea only to have people respond with *impossible!* When people respond with unbelief, the challenges I face become bigger in my thinking. For that reason, I look to people who are always free to say what they think but who also can respond with, *I don't know how that is possible, but let's find a way.* Wisdom's creative expressions fulfill this assignment brilliantly.

EXCELLENCE

Perfectionism is religion, while excellence is Kingdom. Perfectionism is always demanding, yet impossible to satisfy. Excellence is *doing* and *becoming* our best in any situation or task. With excellence of heart, we give the best of our time, efforts, thoughts, prayers, and talents to be fully invested in any responsibility God has given us. Becoming our best means to learn and make whatever changes are necessary to progressively step into new levels of excellence. Every person has access to function in this realm, but it takes effort, discipline, and humility. This basically means that each of us is to make the commitment needed to the lifestyle of excellence, becoming the best that we can become in any given area of life. This is the brilliance of God that becomes the brilliance of humanity. When it comes to talent and skill, our abilities vary. My best may not be as good as your best in any given area of life. Yet for the believer, the heart of excellence is always focused on doing everything *"as unto the Lord* and *with all of my might"* (Col. 3:23). That motivation brings out levels of brilliance in us that can be tapped no other way. An unbeliever could never touch that level of pure motivation. Excellence of heart is truly available for all. And it's from the heart that all these issues of life flow (see Prov. 4:23).

Excellence is sought after and even required by the kings of the earth. That "king" may be a CEO of a corporation or the president of a nation. They all have an appetite for excellence and determine to have it exist all around them. While I believe it's a God-given appetite, I'd never suggest that the way the appetite is expressed is always right.

Proverbs addresses this reality so beautifully:

> *Do you see a man who excels in his work? He will stand before kings; he will not stand before unknown men. When you sit down to eat with a ruler, consider carefully what is before you; and put a knife to your throat if you are a man given to appetite* (Proverbs 22:29-23:2 NKJV).

This reveals several things that are important to us as we seek to create and live in sanctified brilliance. The first is that excellence is the way to promotion. Second is that kings and leaders have an appetite for excellence. Third, if you want to keep your place of influence, put a knife to your throat (self-imposed restriction in your appetite for more). Recognizing your bent to want what others have is the honest evaluation that could save your life in that environment. What this means is that in their world of abundance, you can really only have one of two things—influence or personal gain. Many get promoted because of their excellence in work but lose the excellence of heart in the environment of extreme abundance. Their longing for more (wealth, power, position/title, or fame) causes them to lose their influence in exchange for personal gain. It's not that all gain is wrong. God often brings such abundance into the life of the one who lives faithfully. But there's a great difference when the abundance is the reward versus the goal. Those in power can easily recognize when others are serving them for selfish gain. That *I'll-scratch-your-back-if-you-scratch-mine* attitude is the nature of the political system. It's easy to lose influence by losing the pure heart, as good leaders will never continually subject themselves to the influence of one who serves in order to obtain. That approach to serving usually gives way to manipulation as a viable tool. Excellence in work must mirror the excellence of heart. And it's the excellence in heart that must be protected and sustained in every environment that excellence in work will take us.

INTEGRITY

One of the greatest tragedies in all of history is to have the wisest person to ever live fall into sins of absolute foolishness. By marrying foreign women, Solomon ended up worshiping false gods that these women worshiped in their home countries. He even built temples to these gods in Jerusalem and offered sacrifices to those demonic beings. I've been told it took 300 years for Israel to recover from the effects in culture brought on by the sins of Solomon. It's the responsibility of leaders to realize that their sins will have a negative impact outside of their personal lives. What makes this story even more ironic is that the wisdom that was given to Solomon would have kept him from error had he only lived by what he knew to be true. If ever there was an example of what it is like to know things in the mind that didn't become a personal experience, this is it. Knowledge of truth that is unapplied eventually deadens us to the full impact of those specific truths. Strangely, we become insulated from the conviction of the Holy Spirit concerning the truths we understand the most if they have not impacted our lifestyle. I think it is in part what Paul was referring to when he said *"knowledge puffs up"* (1 Cor. 8:1 NKJV). He didn't say carnal knowledge, nor did he say knowledge about idols or other obvious errors. Knowledge, unapplied, works against God's intended purpose for that knowledge.

Throughout the book of Proverbs are warnings about associating with those given to sin. There's an entire chapter warning the reader to stay away from the immoral (like chapter 7). But he didn't practice what he taught others to do. He instructed us to bind the Word of God to our hearts so we wouldn't fall into sin. He didn't follow through with that, either. My purpose isn't to list Solomon's sins. My intention is to describe how when wisdom is applied to a life, it will manifest in personal integrity.

Wisdom's effects on integrity are seen and measured in our relationships, our thoughts, our ambitions, our use of money, and even where we focus our eyes. All of these things contribute to the integrity of heart, which must be protected at all costs. Once integrity is lost, we have nothing.

What is written in Proverbs about wisdom is not lessened in power because of Solomon's failure. It has quite the opposite effect on my heart, as it becomes extremely sobering to realize we can be given a gift from God but still not benefit from His intended purpose when it is not utilized through complete surrender to Jesus.

CONSTRUCTION HERE AND NOW

Wisdom builds with eternity in mind. It has a present-tense effect with an eternal purpose. Wisdom connects the two worlds of eternity and time in a most unexpected way as we become builders of a heavenly culture with eternal impact here and now. *Arise and build* is the mandate of the hour for us all.

Chapter Six

ALL KINGDOMS BECOME HIS KINGDOM

The Kingdom of God is a present-tense reality. It is manifested wherever the *dominion* of the *King* is realized—king-dom. Practically speaking the Kingdom of God is seen whenever the effects of Jesus' Lordship are demonstrated over the broken issues in life. As those issues of life are transformed through God's redemptive touch, they always manifest the presence of God's Kingdom.

The Kingdom of God is in the unseen world, but it has an effect on the visible. This is illustrated in the ministry of Jesus. When the unseen Kingdom of God was manifested, healing and deliverance were given to people. Those are only two of the manifestations of the Kingdom, and there are countless more. When He performed those miracles, He illustrated the effects of His rule, God's manifested Kingdom. Paul stated, *"The kingdom of God is not meat and drink; but righteousness, and peace, and joy"* (Rom. 14:17 KJV). It is not of the natural world. But as it is for the blind man who now sees, it has become evident through a change in the natural.

The effects of this Kingdom are seen and measurable in what Jesus taught and practiced. As a result, we learn through His example that the Kingdom of God is here. It is now. But truth is often held in tension. That's where seemingly opposite concepts are held together, and they in turn create tension in our thinking. Truth lies in that tension. In this case, it is the fact that the Kingdom of God is present, and yet the fullness of the Kingdom of God cannot be fully realized now, as our bodies could not withstand the glory. And so we live with this reality—the Kingdom of God is both *now and not yet*.

NOW, BUT NOT YET

My point of contention is that for many, the *not yet* has become the hiding place of unbelief. It is the *not yet* that often brings me to the false conclusion that a given breakthrough didn't happen because it wasn't God's will. We might think, "After all, God is big enough and powerful enough to make anything happen that He wants to happen." There's no question of His ability to do whatever He wants. But we are not robots. Nor does He program us like a computer so that His intended purpose is accomplished. Instead, we have been adopted by a perfect Father. He is a Father who longs for sons and daughters to join Him in the family business. These partners are called *co-laborers*. He has servants in the angelic realm as well as the creatures that live around the throne. The book of Revelation gives us a glimpse into this reality. But co-laborers are those who are made in His image, who have a place in His heart that no other part of creation can bear.

Sons and daughters have access to His heart. And as we take advantage of this honor and responsibility, we learn to enforce His will through prayer and obedience. This partnership has an effect on the outcome of things. But when we have fallen short of the example and instruction Jesus gave us, we all too often use the sovereignty of God as our excuse. I have no doubt that there are times when, in His sovereignty, He decides differently than what we had planned or prayed for. But all too often, the beauty and wonder of His sovereignty becomes the carpet under which we sweep unanswered prayers, assuming it was His will to say no to a given request or direction. That just isn't always the case. We have a role to play that influences the outcome.

Those who see no miracles, or very few miracles, use this excuse a lot. Those who live the miracle lifestyle rarely use it, as they have discovered the heart of God on another level. And that level is available to all.

In this journey, I have learned to live with, and enjoy, mystery. I don't need to know why. I just need to know His heart and what He requires of me. As a result, I have chosen not to sacrifice what I know about the goodness of God on the altar of human reasoning so that I can have an explanation for what didn't happen as I expected. Mystery in my life is as important as revelation. If I don't value mystery, I will cut short my opportunities to grow in trust.

THE RELATIONAL JOURNEY

Often, weak theology that looks so good on paper is what becomes the disguise for cowardice, as it pertains to our responsibility in invading the impossible. This in turn keeps us from pursuing what is possible in our lifetime. It's simply much easier to look for explanations for the lack of answers than it is to seek God until there is a breakthrough. The challenging part of this equation is that the answer is not usually a more-correct theology. It is not always in principle. It is in our relationship with Him. It is the readiness to embrace His design by saying yes to this *relational journey*.

Some things only become clear to us through the relationship we have with the Holy Spirit. It is possible to be biblically correct in principle and completely miss what God is saying. Jesus commanded His disciples to go into the whole world and preach the Gospel. When the apostle Paul planned to go to Asia, which fulfills part of the mandate from Scripture, the Holy Spirit said no. Luke writes in Acts 16:6, *"they were forbidden by the Holy Spirit to preach the word in Asia"* (NKJV). When he and his team tried to go Bithynia, the Scriptures said, *"The Spirit did not permit them"* (Acts 16:7 NKJV). It was biblical to go to both locations, but it wasn't the will of God. Their relationship with the Holy Spirit helped them to know the specific will of God for them at that time. It would be incorrect to conclude that God didn't have a heart for certain parts of the world. He just sees the necessary order and process that we don't see. He always leads us to build for the big picture. Later we see the Gospel of the Kingdom made it to Asia with powerful impact. *"All who dwelt in Asia heard the word of the Lord Jesus, both Jews and Greeks"* (Acts 19:10 NKJV).

My favorite example of this kind of biblical conflict is found in Proverbs 26:4-5. Verse 4 says, *"Do not answer a fool according to his folly, lest you also be like him."* And the very next verse brings the contradiction. *"Answer a fool according to his folly, lest he be wise in his own eyes"* (NKJV). So, what command do we follow? He actually told us *not* to speak to the fool, and then told us *to* speak to the fool. The point should become clearer and clearer in our years with Christ that the will of God is revealed in Scripture, but the specifics become known through relationship. It is a relational journey. Obviously, He will never contradict His Word. Yet sometimes His Word seemingly contradicts itself, only to drive us to Him. Again, it's about the relationship. The key for all of us to fulfill our destinies in Christ is centered on our relationship with the Holy Spirit.

The bottom line is, He wants us to display the wonder and the beauty of His will now. It is His will, manifested in the broken circumstances of life, that reveals His Kingdom come and, woven deeply into our church culture, makes us a viable influence in our communities.

Several years ago, we had a local beautician experience a miracle in her body while receiving prayer at Bethel. When one of her customers came in depressed, she asked what was up. The client mentioned she had just been diagnosed with cancer. The beautician said she needed to get down to Bethel, as they don't tolerate cancer. She did. And she was healed.

I love that story. I wish I could say that everyone we pray for with that horrible disease has been healed. It's not true at all. We've had tragic losses. But we are in the journey, contending for a *cancer-free zone,* as that is the nature of His world. How could we pursue anything less?

The question remains: how much of God's Kingdom can we experience now?

HOW MUCH NOW?

We're in a journey to discover, experience, and release the reality of His rule here and now. Is it correct to expect more? If so, how much can we expect? Here are some personal conclusions on the subject:

1. We couldn't survive the full expression of God's Kingdom here on earth because His glory is a manifestation of His Kingdom. The fullness of His glory is beyond what the human body can endure. So the *not yet* has merit. Only glorified bodies can handle the full manifestation of His Kingdom.

2. We can have more than we presently have. History tells us that much. Church history is filled with stories that are far beyond what most of us have experienced here and now. Even Israel experienced measures of His presence unheard of today, all while under an inferior covenant. To see *the more* that existed in history and not cry out for great increase is biblically unreasonable.

3. He gave us a direction in prayer that is beyond all we could *ask or think,* which means it's beyond our faith

and imagination. That prayer, *"on earth as it is in heaven,"* is both a command and an invitation. Obeying the command to pray, followed by risk-oriented actions needed to experience what He declared to be His will, enables us to discover things we never would have had the intelligence or spiritual discernment to ask for.

4. Jesus didn't set a boundary, saying, "Believe for this much, but no more." He set a direction in teaching and action, but never set the boundaries that present-day leaders set for us. In fact, to give us the hope and courage we'd need, He announced that we would to do greater works than He did. We can't do greater until we've done the same. He is inviting us into a profound exploration of what it looks like when His Kingdom becomes more fully manifest now.

5. He set a direction for our hope by declaring, *"The kingdoms of this world have become the kingdoms of our Lord and of His Christ"* (Rev. 11:15 NKJV). And yet again He said the glory of the Lord will *cover the earth* (see Hab. 2:14). These two statements reveal the measurable target of His will and disclose the anticipation of His heart.

Because Jesus set a seemingly impossible ideal for us in prayer and because He didn't set boundaries, how could we give ourselves to anything less than a full expression of God's dominion realized over the whole earth? None of us have been given a strategy on how that is supposed to happen apart from following the example that Jesus gave us by *"destroying the works of the evil one"* (see 1 John 3:8). We were given a direction, a prayer, a commission, and an example to follow. And all of that is given to us without restraints.

I understand that what I have encouraged will make some nervous. In history, there were those who tried to create God's Kingdom on earth, sometimes calling their project Zion or some other biblical name. But in each case, they met with failure. It appears to me that they may have failed because they placed themselves at the top of the hierarchical system, and that was their idea of His Kingdom come to earth. It's important for us to serve at whatever level He requires of us, but to let all positions of rule or influence be the promotion of the Lord and not self-promotion. The surest way for us to fall short is to promote ourselves.

So how do we carry this mandate responsibly? Hope is at the root.

THE ISSUE IS HOPE

At this point, many will warn about giving false hope. That possibility is very real and painful. When false hope is given, it is usually in the context of hype, which I despise. It promises miracles, breakthroughs, fulfilled dreams, and perhaps even material blessing in the name of faith. But it can't deliver. I do think it is often a carnal attempt at faith and sometimes well intended. Hype is dishonest at its root. Those who live this way lose credibility over time. Yet my concern and focus is more on our not giving people an inferior or weak hope. Both caution and fear are often called wisdom by those unwilling to live with the level of risk necessary to bring about significant advancements in our Kingdom lifestyle and experience. Whenever weakness in faith is given a virtuous name, it has permission to stay.

Several years ago, one of the young mothers in the church, Olivia Shupe, came out of a time of prayer with a message that has impacted our environment for quite a while now. She said the Lord said to her, "The one with the most hope has the most influence." This is one of the most important things we can learn about our lives. They must be lived with hope in every area. In fact, any area of our life that has no hope is under the influence of a lie.

*Now may the God of hope fill you with all joy and peace
in believing, so that you will abound in hope by the power
of the Holy Spirit* (Romans 15:13).

Hope is to affect everything! Our approach to the past must be through the blood of Jesus. I am as clean as Jesus, as I stand before the Father washed in the blood of the Lamb. Our approach to the present is to be as sons and daughters who know they are forgiven and now must live responsibly to see His Kingdom come to every part of life. Our approach to the future is to lay down our lives so that what He has intended to happen on the earth will, in fact, happen, and we will have received our assignment in shaping the course of history responsibly. Hope joyfully takes people to breakthroughs otherwise unattainable.

HOW THEN DO WE LIVE?

As a group of believers, we have purposed to live with the idea that the Gospel is perfectly suited for every area of life. It is practical and needed. In His wisdom, He has solutions for every problem and has a heart for every person. Our approach is inspired by the verse that states He is *"the Desire of All Nations"* (Hag. 2:7 NKJV). In other words, everyone wants a king like Jesus. He is what everyone longs for; they just don't know it. As such, Jesus is perfectly suited to give influence, meaning, and significance for all aspects of life.

We recently celebrated the 500-year anniversary of the Reformation. The leaders of that day were successful in shaping their culture because they believed God had answers for every part of life. It didn't matter if it was banking, or business, or education, or science, and so on. The point is this Gospel is designed to bring the reality of the Kingdom into every part of life. And in doing so, people are fulfilled in purpose. The people of God must embrace the privilege of living in the open, regardless of the field of influence, so that the reality of God's Kingdom is recognizable. Remember, He said, *"Taste and see that the Lord is good"* (Ps. 34:8). *Taste* is experience. *See* is perception. Once people experience the reality of the Kingdom, their perception will change. Give them a taste.

Chapter Seven

PEACE IS THE OXYGEN OF HEAVEN

M ost of what we want to be a prevailing influence in a culture begins with one person. When any individual touches the reality of Heaven and brings that influence into their family and/or to closest friends, or even a work environment, they start having an impact on their surroundings. That family or group then helps to shape the values of an entire local church. And when the Church begins to illustrate the reality of another world, it is positioned to influence a city. The point is, culture isn't shaped because we take on a "culture campaign." It usually starts with one person, or perhaps a small group of people of like mind, who model, teach, and monitor the atmosphere for the sake of others. It is this heavenly reality that God has designed to influence earth until we see the fulfillment of the prayer *"on earth as it is in heaven."*

PEACE

For most people, peace is a time without war, or a time without conflict, or as simple as a time without noise. Take note that it's always the absence of something. In the Kingdom of God, peace is the presence of someone. Peace is a person. Jesus is the Prince of Peace. When the prevailing influence on our hearts and minds is the presence of Jesus, we have peace that conquers. The wonderful reality of this kind of peace is that it is not defined or controlled by its surroundings. This kind of peace changes its surroundings. Jesus slept in a storm and then released peace over that storm, and the storm stopped (see Mark 4:35-41). What was in Him influenced what happened around Him.

FELT REALITIES

Most every believer lives with the knowledge that the Holy Spirit lives in him or her and that He will never leave. That knowledge is a vital biblical truth. But truth is to be known by experience. Religion idolizes concepts but avoids personal experience. Knowing He is my provider is reassuring. But it does me little good if I don't seek Him for provision. The concept of salvation does me no good unless I'm saved. Being born again is the experience we have after receiving the message of salvation. And so, the abiding presence of the Holy Spirit must become a felt reality.

Many will think I mean we are to live by our emotions, or that our emotions define what is true. That would certainly lead to another set of problems. While that is true, a felt reality will usually affect my emotions. It had better be real enough to affect part of my life. Everything about us, from our minds to our emotions to our physical bodies, is designed to recognize and dwell in the manifest presence of God. Learning how to live in that reality is called maturity (see Heb. 5:12-14).

We must put a demand on our faith and stop allowing complacency to define our life in Christ. The idea of the Holy Spirit abiding with us always must affect how we do life. And that life can be lived with a consciousness of Him that He affects faith, attitudes, conduct, and so much more. He is the pleasure of life.

We often speak of using faith for a miracle, which is right and good. But what if we were to also use our faith to discover *God with us?*

PROTECTING PEACE

Peace is the atmosphere of Heaven. I like to call peace the *oxygen of Heaven.* And that peace is with me constantly. But if I violate that peace through fear, anger, or other such contradictions to His nature, it is no longer a felt reality. I'm not saying the Holy Spirit left me. I'm just saying that peace no longer benefits me. It's no longer something that I draw from and can steward well. Perhaps I could put it this way: Because He will never leave me, peace is in my account, but it's not in my possession. I need to make a withdrawal.

One of the most important principles I live by is to protect my peace at all costs. That means when I find that I'm without it, I have to find out where I left it. It's that simple. When I feel anxious or frustrated, I try to figure out how long I have allowed inferior realities to influence my thoughts, attitudes, and behavior. If, for example, I recognize I've been anxious for about three hours, then I'll look to what triggered it. Perhaps it was a phone call. This doesn't mean the phone call was wrong. But my reaction may have been. As a result, I gave way to fear by what I thought about. All of our responses either come from love or fear. So I look back to the phone call and begin to see more clearly how I gave fear a place in my heart and mind. Perhaps I started to think of all the wrong that could happen. Remember, fear thinks apart from promise. It could have been a call about anything—a personal challenge, or something happening in the church, or even a report about a national or international crisis. The issue is, I exchanged peace for fear. And it was a bad deal. I traded something eternal for something that works its way into our lives only to steal, kill, and destroy.

When I see what has happened, I repent. I make full confession to the Lord. If it's an ongoing issue, my repentance must be more deeply expressed. Honestly, sometimes seeing the problem is all it takes. I follow that with a simple prayer of confession:

> *Jesus, forgive me. I allowed fear to challenge my knowledge of Your goodness. Thank You for Your forgiveness as I know You will be my strength when the next problem appears. I give You thanks and praise, for You're always good.*

It's so beautiful, as peace is now restored. I can't create it. It's already my possession. I just need to get it out of my account and back into my possession. But other times I can tell the problem is much more deeply rooted in me. In a moment of God's dealings, we see that perhaps there's a root of wrong thinking that has influenced our lives for years. In that case, it's time to get alone with the Lord so that I am certain that my repentance is as deep as my sin. I look to the Scriptures to find what He says about me, my problem, and what His answer is for what has caused me to stumble. It's important that I find where I was ignorant of truth, or perhaps mishandled truth through my unbelief. Regardless of how long that takes, whether it's ten minutes or an hour, it's worth it to not have to carry the burden of *deception in thought* around any longer. Wrong thinking doesn't coexist with peace. Repentance, changing the way we think, restores our peace.

PROTECTED BY PEACE

Living in peace is a relational journey with the Holy Spirit. That journey is at its best when we have an absolute trust in God, demonstrated through abiding in Christ. When I embrace fear, I am doubting God. Our entire life on this planet is about learning to trust the One who is perfectly faithful and trustworthy. Our reasoning, apart from divine influence, always wars against this One who is worthy of our trust. And that is the battle. It's a battle in the mind, to spoil and infect our hearts. Winning this battle affects every area of life.

The apostle Paul faced some of the most extreme experiences that one could face. And it was from prison he wrote some of the most helpful insights for our lives.

> *Rejoice in the Lord always; again I will say, rejoice! ... Be anxious for nothing, but in everything by prayer and supplication with thanksgiving let your requests be made known to God. And the peace of God, which surpasses all comprehension, will guard your hearts and your minds in Christ Jesus* (Philippians 4:4-7).

Rejoicing, prayer, supplication, and thanksgiving all help to settle the battle for our minds. In the verse that follows (Phil. 4:8) Paul gives us insight on what to fill our minds with. The implication is that if it is filled with the things of God, there will be no room for thoughts that violate our view of His nature. And whenever we discover His nature, we also discover our new nature in Christ. We always become like the One we trust.

It is important to pray, bringing our needs, fears, and challenges to God. He welcomes us in any state we are in. But the prayers of authority are never prayed in fear. Fear-based prayers are the prayers of servants, not sons and daughters. Again, He welcomes me in whatever condition I am in. In His mercy, He ministers to us and heals us. But He has called us into a lifestyle that is much higher than that. I encourage people to pray until the fear and anxiety are gone. For me this process always involves worship and feeding my heart on the promises of God. As we return to a place of faith, we become useful co-laborers in making the decrees necessary to bring about God's will in a given situation. Giving thanks is what helps to keep us in tune with our Father who never lies and is always worthy of our trust. Thankfulness flows effortlessly from the one who has experienced this internal victory.

The part of the passage I want to look at again is, *"And the peace of God, which surpasses all comprehension, will guard your hearts and your minds"* (Phil. 4:7). It's interesting that if I protect my peace, His peace will protect me. Perhaps it sounds like a contradiction. But it isn't. If I protect my heart from all the things that violate my trust in Him, He will rise up to protect me from the unseen fiery darts headed in my direction. His peace protects us where we lack understanding. It's beautiful to see that peace goes beyond comprehension, as real faith is always superior to natural reasoning. I like to put it this way: If I give up my right to understand, He will give me the peace that passes understanding.

LIFESTYLE PEACE

If I'm going to have a lifestyle of peace, I have to make decisions about my approach to life. Many people live from the stresses of life, as that motivates them to be focused and get things accomplished. They are intentional in their use of negative influence. That means they live in reaction to problems instead of in response to the purposes of God. I'm not saying it doesn't work. Stress can move people into action to get things done. But peace is too important for me to give that exterior motivator a place in my heart. I may gain productivity, but what I lose is of utmost importance to me—the felt reality of His presence. I have chosen to live in response to the Father, and not in reaction to darkness. I value felt presence more than I value accomplishing what seems to impress others the most. The wonderful reality is that living from presence enables us to accomplish that which will last.

Protecting my peace must get practical. For example, I won't read any challenging emails or engage in difficult conversations late at night, if it's at all possible to avoid. I don't want those things to become the meditation of my heart as I go to sleep. Most people would have better days if they had better nights. As a pastor, I sometimes find this unavoidable. Crisis happens. When it does, we all have to respond to these things with a heart of a servant and a heart full of faith. But to constantly entertain ideas, problems, and conflicts late at night, when they could be handled better the next day, is to tempt God. I owe Him a clean heart of affection as I go to sleep. This is a heart that is not cluttered with the debris of unsettled things. Our nights are the time when the Holy Spirit ministers to us in ways that are far beyond what we can handle during the day. It's important to enter the night of rest in a way that positions us to receive from God. Fear often repels His work.

For me a clean conscience is more than being free from the awareness of sin in my life. It is being free from the weightiness of life that entangles my heart, prohibiting me from the life of faith for which I was designed. A clean conscience is a heart at rest.

For those times when conflict is unavoidable, I have had to learn how to pray into a place where fear doesn't dictate what and whom I trust. What I mean by that is, I pray until I have effectively placed my burden into His care. I know when I have succeeded, as I'm no longer anxious. That is the posture of rest. And thankfulness flows easily from that place.

A heart at rest is a heart of faith. I'm not just talking about sleep, as exhausted people can sleep even though they're not in a place of trusting God. Rest is a place where we refuse to strive. Faith doesn't come from striving. It comes from surrender. And that is the place of great peace.

RELATIONSHIPS OF PEACE

I know people who will overemphasize a problem, hoping to get me to become anxious with them. Honestly. That's how they seem to know that I see the problem is as critical as they view it to be. The logic behind this is that anxiousness and fear show we're serious about the problem and completely awake to the need of the moment. If I'm anxious and fretting, then they know I am with them. One of the important Kingdom truths is that perfect love drives out fear. Showing compassion to the one in crises is the answer. Feel their pain, and learn to mourn with those who mourn. And don't take their problem lightly. Pray with them when the time is right. Comfort them. Encourage them. Talk only when necessary. But don't sacrifice your peace to prove you're with them. Faith rests. It is also true that faith fights. But it fights from the position of rest/confidence in God. In this setting, complacency becomes counterfeit peace. Faith is. And I'm no good to my friend if I'm as fearful as they are. My prayers will then become begging sessions, not prayers of authority that God has designed us for.

When peace is the agreed-upon value of a community of believers who are contending for *"on earth as it is in heaven,"* they will not use fear to control or influence others. This is so deeply rooted in our culture that people often seem to be unaware of using this tool to manipulate others to their need or point of view. Politicians do this a lot. Most of our media outlets live off of the money produced by fear. Preachers often do the same, as do parents. Heaven's culture doesn't allow us to use instruments of fear, as fear is inferior to and undermines real faith.

Problems exist. Seeing them from God's perspective is the safest way to survive, thrive, and overcome in the days we live in.

DENIAL, COUNTERFEIT FAITH

There are many who are unable to discuss a problem because for them it is a sign of unbelief. Real faith can stand up to any challenge and any subject. But it must be anchored in the One who is faithful.

Faith doesn't deny a problem's existence. It denies it a place of influence. Honest conversation, expressing needs, fears, and the like, must be welcome in the family of God. We are growing into a mature representation of Jesus, and process must be allowed and celebrated. This is especially true for young believers. Mocking someone for weak faith never creates great faith. But a faith culture must understand that when people are overcome by their challenges in life, we must not mirror their fear to prove we're with them. To be a part of the answer, be the loving support that functions out of peace.

Jesus often spoke to people about their unbelief. Once again, He never withheld a miracle because of weak faith or unbelief. If they had enough faith to come to Him, He responded to their need as the Father's redemptive solution. It seems to me He addressed their unbelief so that after the miracle came, they could step into greater faith.

The issue of faith was of much more importance to Jesus than to most of us. Jesus was so concerned about this issue that He asked if He would find any on the earth when He returned.

WHEN WE DON'T UNDERSTAND

The bottom line is that mystery is a huge part of the disciple's life. That's why we're given promises about all things working for good. And He will complete what He started. Faith works in tandem with peace. Faith satisfies the appetite of the questioning heart when understanding is missing. It is substance.

One of the things that makes room for the spirit of revelation to come is that we are willing to embrace mystery. What you don't understand is as important as what you do understand. If a person who has been given tremendous revelation and an equally weighty mystery can walk in the call of God by revelation and not be pulled off by the mystery (the inability to answer important questions), that person will discover the richness of the call of God.

Chapter Eight

ERASING LINES

The Church is typically able to set standards for worship, morality, and compassion that certainly remind people how we're to do life. But even then, these values tend to get locked up in the four walls of the buildings in which we gather, instead of actually influencing the value system of the cities we live in. While this is a good start, it falls short of the intention of the Lord when He stated that we are the *"salt of the earth* (Matt. 5:13).

Salt in Jesus' illustration is about adding flavor to a community in the same way salt is used to enhance the flavor of a meal. Consider the profound effect Jesus speaks of in this metaphor. We are *added* to the meal, implying we are not the whole meal. The Church tends to think that we are complete and the city needs us. While that has merit, it's truer to say that we are to be added to what already exists by God's design. Another way to express the same concept is to say that the whole Church is in the Kingdom, but the whole Kingdom isn't in the Church. He works profoundly through people who do not yet know Him. We demonstrate wisdom when we recognize that simple fact and honor them accordingly.

The way we typically apply the principle of being the salt of the earth would look like us unscrewing the lid of the salt shaker and pouring all the contents on the corner of the plate. That illustrates our desire to stay together. As long as our flavor (influence) is only experienced by other believers, we have little influence outside of the church. And while we must not forsake the corporate gathering with others in the faith, our ability to bring influence to our surroundings comes when we become evenly sprinkled over the whole meal (our community). In other words, our time together is to equip us for our influence in the community when we're not together.

We must give attention to the fact that Jesus is erasing the lines of separation in several areas of our thinking and in our values. These lines are ones that we made, not Him. Erasing these lines ultimately affects our behavior. In doing so, it helps to lift the veil that keeps the Church hidden from the healthy influence we were born to bring to the city around us.

SECULAR AND SACRED

I grew up at a time when those who were pastors, missionaries, and evangelists were considered to be *in the ministry*. They had sacred assignments because of their obvious responsibility to preach the Gospel. It seemed to escape our notice that every believer living the Gospel in the everyday affairs of life wasn't considered as important as preaching. Nor was there the same value for those with occupations that were not overtly spiritual. The thought that every believer was in ministry regardless of their occupation was foreign to most.

I remember so clearly when my dad and pastor began to teach that every believer was a priest unto the Lord (see 1 Pet. 2:9). This concept had been bantered around for centuries, but it has never really taken root in the measure that God intended. We needed to hear it again, this time at a whole new level.

That every believer was a priest unto the Lord was such a profound insight that it changed our lives completely. It started with the concept of worship. We learned that it was our privilege to minister to God with thanksgiving and praise and offer ourselves to Him in worship. It took a while, but soon the Church was truly embracing our assignment to minister to God. But still the line remained in people's thinking as it pertained to employment. That's the line that said one job was secular and the other was spiritual. For example, if someone worked in a school as a teacher of children, it was admired but was not considered spiritual. The same was true of any other occupation outside of public ministry.

In reality, there is no secular job for a believer. In all honesty, I've met people whose approach to their job in business is more holy than some I've known in their approach to pastoring. It's not the task that makes it holy. It is holy entirely based on the One who called us to that task, giving us His commission. His call is always holy. My approach to the call determines my effectiveness. Once we say yes to the responsibility, it is sanctified by the One who gave us the assignment. I would never want to lower the esteem given to the missionary, etc. I simply want to raise the value for all who have said yes to the call of God, whether it is full-time evangelistic work or to be a missionary, or a dentist, or a stay-at-home mom. Saying yes to God is the big deal. It is the daily yes to God that sanctifies the work.

My dear friend, Winkie Pratney, has done a brilliant job of helping us to see the spiritual nature of what the Church has called secular. In his recent book, *Spiritual Vocations*, he describes the spirituality of all legitimate vocations by showing that each one originated with God Himself. For example, God was the first gardener, the first artist, the first coach, the first counselor, the first lawyer, the first doctor, the first builder, etc. This realization helps us to see that our assignments in life have great spiritual significance, whether or not we stand behind pulpits. For the One who is perfect in holiness first manifested these skills to reveal how He thinks and what He values. In these jobs, we have the privilege of representing and mirroring the heart and nature of God in all we do. It frees us to have an intentional approach to our responsibilities, knowing that adding our faith to what we do can bring about such profound transformation to every area that is under our influence. But it ultimately positions us for the next reformation, as this could help bring the influence of King Jesus into every sphere of influence in society. We desperately need people who are filled with the Holy Spirit in politics, entertainment, medicine, education, etc. Only then will the effect that Jesus spoke of be realized when He said, *"the kingdom of heaven is like leaven"* (Matt. 13:33). Leaven is quiet, subtle, evenly spread out, and powerfully effective to everything it touches. That is the influence of the Kingdom of God on the world around us as we give ourselves to serve in any capacity for which He calls us.

This part of our culture is essential, as it empowers each believer to become what God intended, with an eternal purpose. Godly self-esteem increases as we realize we are in our role by divine assignment. The fruit of this posture is not only life-changing; it influences culture itself. This is why He is truly erasing the line between secular and sacred.

THE VEIL IS TORN

When the Church experiences Heaven's culture, the Lord lifts the veil that separates the two worlds—church and community. It's much like when He tore the veil in the temple at the death of Christ. It was that veil that separated His reality from ours. It was the resurrection of Jesus that made *"Heaven on earth"* even a possibility as the normal Christian life. When this happens, it's the Lord Himself who lets the world take a peek at the way His world functions.

Jesus is called *"the Desire of All Nations."* The implication is that everyone wants a king like Jesus. He oversees a Kingdom where everyone is not only safe but is also completely fulfilled in their reason for being. In this Kingdom, everyone has value, is celebrated, and functions according to their gifts in a way that benefits the whole. This is the nature of His world that can be experienced by anyone who makes Jesus Lord (King) over their life.

As the Church learns to live in Heaven's culture here and now, everyone wins. And the principles of that Kingdom are usable in every part of society. A better term is "transferable." For example, the way people are valued and honored in the Kingdom of God will actually work in any business or political office in the world. It works beautifully in the church, but also in the medical community and our schools. His culture in the *Kingdom-oriented* church is transferable to every part of society.

The alternative is a sad reality. For example, if we were to take the common church culture as it applies to money and transfer that culture to a major company like Apple Computer, they would face unusual challenges in a short period of time. This is because what will work in a church, whether it's a church of 200 or 20,000, will not necessarily work outside of the people who invented it. Here is the reality: Agreed-upon values can work as long as the people affected agree. This is true even if they're inferior to good or right values. On the other hand, the values of the Kingdom of God work everywhere. The principle of lordship or kingship brings out His nature in all He designed.

Discovering the value system of Heaven gives us access to influence the systems of this world. I remind you that it is our Savior's goal for all the kingdoms of this world to become the Kingdom of our God. Don't make the mistake of putting that promise off into a period of time for which we have no responsibility. We tend to do that with promises that require great faith. We must pursue this in prayer for our lifetime to display our loyalty to His heart.

As we live with His values and give place to His atmosphere (which in reality is His presence/face), God lifts the veil of separation that His people might have influence over what lies beyond the four walls of the church.

NATURAL AND SUPERNATURAL

Many parts of the world have a high value for the supernatural. It's in their culture. That doesn't mean that their understanding is correct. But they usually don't have resistance to the authentic when it's presented. The Church in the western world has backed so far away from this biblical culture that it's frightening. In its place, we have created a lifestyle that we can understand and control. In doing so, we often end up with a rather tame god made in our own image, one we can manage, who seldom offends us. In spite of this, there has always been a remnant. And although they are usually scorned by their own brothers and sisters, they have courageously paved the way for what we're experiencing now—an increase of signs, wonders, and miracles—a supernatural lifestyle that brings honor to Jesus. He is the only One worth following.

Most every group I encounter in these days, regardless of denominational affiliation, has an increasing hunger for biblical Christianity, with passion for both power and purity. This has brought the supernatural activities of God back to the forefront. It's beautiful and wonderful, with fruit that glorifies the name of Jesus.

It is exciting to see the culture of the Church change, being influenced by an awareness of our God, for whom nothing is impossible. That awareness changes everything. But we are still natural people, living in a natural world. Seeing this apparent dichotomy between the natural and supernatural realms, we need God's heart to value them responsibly. We have two realms that we're aware of—natural and supernatural. God only has one—the natural. Think about this: The supernatural is His natural, and He made the natural, so it is also His natural realm. The natural realm is not evil. It mirrors the heavenly realm in profound ways. And when He's at work, they flow together seamlessly.

What we sometimes don't understand is how much God values the natural world. When He was leading Israel out of Egypt into the Promised Land, He took them through the wilderness. In the wilderness, He was manifested among them through the pillar of fire by night and the cloud during the day. They entered the wilderness through two walls of water as the Red Sea split in two and then came crashing back together to destroy the Egyptian army that tried to capture and kill them. Manna appeared on the ground daily, except for the Sabbath. For on the sixth day, God provided double the manna so they'd have enough to eat on the day of rest without having to gather it (work). Water was provided for them out of a rock. On and on these stories go, as God sustained them through miracles. But He was taking them to the Promised Land, where they'd have to work for food. In most of our thinking, the idea of God supernaturally supplying our need is the picture of the Promised Land. But it wasn't to God. He wanted them trained in the supernatural through unusual provision so that they would grow in their trust of Him. In turn, He could then trust them with the abundant supply He intended for them in the Promised Land.

Remember, His heart is to have co-laborers—people with whom He can partner to express His heart and nature in the earth. He wanted them to be faithful to their assignment and work hard, and then to let Him breathe on their labors so they would experience supernatural supply through increase and blessing. Their crops would then produce more than what was natural; their cattle would remain healthy and produce great increase. The fact is, the supernatural God worked with their natural labors to illustrate His heart for mingling His efforts with Israel's. Trusting Him with little to nothing, as Israel did in this story, was a school to train them to do a good job in stewarding God's abundance. The same is true for us today. Lack is the school for abundance if we trust, surrender our labors, and believe in His intention to bless us.

Many today don't want to work and just trust God for provision. That may sound spiritual, but it's not necessarily true. Those people generally live off of the compassion of others as they give them money so they can eat and pay rent. The one who receives the money usually calls it living by faith. (I know that God has actually called some to this lifestyle, and I honor that. But they usually don't broadcast their needs so that people will feel responsible to take care of them.)

I've watched business people who have the responsibility for hundreds of employees. They carry the needs of their families in their hearts. Their faith is stretched to a level that most of us will never experience. Look at is this way—what takes greater faith? Is it to believe for my family's needs every month through the generosity of others, or to believe God for His favor and blessing on my business so that the needs of hundreds of families are met? I believe the latter. Our supernatural Father longs to partner with the natural world that we live in so that the two are perfectly merged in our perspective and in our thinking, all under the Lordship of Jesus.

Another great example is from Proverbs 21:31: *"The horse is prepared for the day of battle, but victory belongs to the Lord."* The horse is the natural. It represents hard work through training and readiness, elements He considers necessary. But the victory is entirely the result of God's intervention. It is supernatural. The natural and supernatural are to work in partnership. God wants our efforts to be unto Him, so that efforts will openly be for us. We must give Him something to breathe on, something to multiply, as He did with the boy's lunch (see John 6:9-14).

As we grow in this journey, we will learn to celebrate natural breakthroughs in the same way we would an obvious miracle. If the Lord were to drop a thousand dollars out of the air to meet my need, or someone gave me the opportunity to earn it through labor, both are supernatural in that God provided both opportunities. One is harder to celebrate because it's possible for me to take credit for it. Maturity sees both as from God and celebrates His grace accordingly. It isn't just seeing God's hand in the creative miracle. It is in the slightest intervention of God in a matter for which we give Him glory. There is a seamless connection between these two realities. It is important to see that God's intention is to make them one, partners together to reveal the heart of a perfect Father. And what is so beautiful about this change in perspective is we will begin to see the hand of our supernatural God at work inside the natural realm more clearly. Our maturity will make us more trustworthy in stewarding the supernatural well, whether or not it is an obvious miracle or the subtle influence of God in a matter.

US AND THEM

There is a great difference between a believer and an unbeliever. The two have completely different natures. One carries the presence of the Holy Spirit; the other doesn't. One has a legitimate hope for eternity; the other doesn't. One has an identity in God, a purpose for being alive, and a destiny. The other doesn't. The believer is set apart for the Lord Himself. So my comments in this section must be taken in light of what I've just mentioned.

Having said that, in a very real sense, God is erasing the line between the world and us. By making every job spiritual, He has given us both the responsibility and the privilege of being sprinkled into a godless world system to love, serve, and bring influence. He who is in us is greater, so there is no fear. But here is the challenge—no one wants to be the project of a Christian who needs to ease his or her conscience by witnessing to and trying to convert an unbeliever. Evangelism is vital! Evangelism is beautiful! But no one wants to be our project.

I have found that people want to be valued. They long to be heard and understood. Everyone longs for friends who can give without requiring anything in return. The bottom line is people want to be loved. And what better way to bring people into the Kingdom than to love them for who they are. This isn't to replace the wonderful role of preaching the Gospel. It's to put it in the context of valuing people before they could earn it.

As Jesus sprinkles us into the world, like salt over a meal, He puts us into contact with all kinds of people. When we enter that environment as a powerful servant, not as an elitist, we resemble Jesus.

Christians often enter certain realms of city life to bring change. That in itself is called vision, which is inspired by hope. We rightfully call that good. An example of this is when someone volunteers at the local school to bring change in their curriculum. Others will volunteer at the local hospital to pray for the sick or influence the doctors and nurses. These desires are wonderful, as we are here to bring change. But agenda-driven relationships often become controlling, and all too easily they can cross the line into manipulation. That is where good becomes evil, and we don't even recognize how and when that happened. Driven people fall into this the most easily as they often run over people to accomplish their task. And yet those without Christ recognize it easily and instinctively war against it.

Through the years, I've had some from our church family move from our city to another and ask me how they can best bring change to the church they will now be attending. I tell them not to try to bring change if they're not the one in charge. Just be quiet and serve. While the desired fruit of our influence in each of these illustrations is legitimate, people can tell whenever anyone comes to help with an agenda. The world often rejects us in that scenario. And then we ignorantly count it as suffering for the Lord, when in fact we're suffering because we're foolish. Everyone has a God-given defense mechanism to protect them and their responsibilities from invaders. And sometimes that invader is a well-intentioned believer who is trying to bring change. But lasting change doesn't usually come through the methods used by Christians who need another notch on their Bibles for a job well done. The worst part of this story is that sometimes we win battles this way. But ultimately, we end up losing the war. Change that lasts happens through those who learn to love. These are the ones who serve with the heart of a king and rule with the heart of a servant.

The best thing we can do is to love people for who they are now and serve, expecting nothing in return. We have given millions of dollars to our city in money and in service and have never asked for anything in return. Not even our own city knows what we've done as most of it has been the *"gift in secret"* (Prov. 21:14). It's for our city, not to improve public opinion. And we never will use our gifts to ask for favors from our city leaders. We give because we love our city.

Churches are known to be agenda driven and, in the process, make enemies. These *enemies* often haven't rejected Jesus. They've rejected us. That changes when we love people for who they are and serve them accordingly.

THE WRONG SPIRIT

Many believers are now seeing that they have a responsibility to bring influence to the world around them. It's beautiful. The testimonies from those who have embarked on such a challenging journey encourage me tremendously. Tragically, quite a number of visionaries become driven in their approach, thinking that God will honor the *"arm of flesh"* (2 Chron. 32:8) as they war for personal significance. It's important for us to realize that God often values our journey more than the outcome. In other words, my responses to His directives along the way are of greater value to Him than is anything I can accomplish through my position of significance or influence.

You may find this offensive, but I have found that God will actually honor the efforts of the unbeliever before honoring the self-centered efforts of His children. He refuses to feed that part of the heart that nourishes itself on flesh in the name of the Spirit. For me, a warning light goes off whenever I see people who are driven toward a spiritual goal. Underlying such an approach is usually an individual whose identity is wrapped up in personal accomplishments instead of in the Name of the One who called us to Himself. I believe the Kingdom has an alternate response to the mandate of the Lord. It is to be focused instead of driven. I keep myself safe by making sure that my pursuit of His purpose for my life is never stronger than my surrender.

WHO IS IN CHARGE?

It should be stated that this isn't about believers being in control of everything. I don't think that would be good for us or for the world around us. It's about the people of God having influence, the kind that brings out the existing greatness of individuals and institutions.

Some of the people who illustrate this best in Scripture are Daniel, Joseph, and Esther. None of them were in charge of their nations. They were not the king, president, prime minister, or any other such dignitary. And while those roles are wonderful to be in if God gives the promotion, the goal is never control. It's influence. These three Old Testament leaders held positions that were not on the top of the ladder of their day. They served the ones who had the responsibility to rule. They served the one at the top. As a result, several nations were spared great calamity, simply because of the influence of those who served.

ERASING TO BUILD

God erases in order to rewrite. He is building His heart and mind into us so that our co-laboring role is never diminished or compromised. And whenever these values become entrenched in the thinking and values of an individual, family, or church, we experience another level of the culture of Heaven. This shift in perspective enables us to be brokers of another world, releasing the reality of His world into this, in part fulfilling our prayer commission for *on earth as it is in heaven.*

Chapter Nine

JESUS, UNAFRAID OF THE SECULAR

Having respect for the world, before their conversion, is an unusually important value. That is not to say that we treasure ungodliness, carnality, or any such thing. It's just wise to recognize the hand of God at work in environments we have little to no influence in. Honoring the person God honors is always important. Religious bias and arrogance keep us from that at times, but it can become a part of our *mode of operation* if changes are made in our thinking.

Understanding this one concept would have helped me navigate many of the controversial issues in church life through the years. Jesus simply thought differently from us. Differently from *all* of us.

The sanctifying presence and power of God changes the equation for us all in our dealings with the world around us. It used to be that the only safe place for the believer was to be separate from everyone who didn't live righteously. And while there is wisdom in staying away from those whose goal it is to bring you down, there's much to be said about the impact we can have because God's power and presence is a felt reality in and through the life of a believer. My favorite illustration once again is—when you touched a leper in the Old Testament, you became unclean. But in the New Testament, Jesus touched the leper and the leper became clean. Jesus has now given us the commission to do the same. In the Old Testament, a person is to stay away from angry people. In the New Testament, a believing spouse sanctifies the life of the unbelieving spouse. It's the effect of the presence and power of God in the believer on their surroundings.

WORDS AND THEIR ORIGINS

Words and their origins can have great meaning for us. Studying them can be quite an enlightening task. I think anyone who has read the Bible would agree with me that certain words carry extra special meaning. This is especially true of the New Testament, where God's plan for the ages unfolds.

I want to address three specific words because none of these words are Hebrew in origin. They were not taken from the rich Jewish heritage that was all around them. They were borrowed from a very secular society. And it was Jesus who chose to use these words that would help to explain what He was doing or was about to do.

These three words are *apostle, church*, and *Paul.* Each of these reveals something very significant in God's plan for the ages. And the side note is that God is not afraid of secular connotations in releasing His message. He is the creator of all nations and often hides His purposes inside the cultures of people we think He would never use. But He does. And we are the ones who need to change our perspective.

The first word, *apostle,* is used in light of the Disciples' Prayer. It is, once again:

> *Our Father who is in heaven,*
> *Hallowed be Your name.*
> *Your kingdom come.*

Your will be done,
On earth as it is in heaven.
Give us this day our daily bread.
And forgive us our debts, as we also have forgiven
our debtors.
And do not lead us into temptation, but deliver
us from evil. [For Yours is the kingdom and the
power and the glory forever. Amen]
(Matthew 6:9-13).

Understanding the purpose and nature of the apostle, and their assignment in society, will help us to appreciate with much greater insight and conviction the reason behind this prayer.

Apostle[4]

Apostle is a term that much of the Church rejects as they don't believe the office still exists today. On the other hand, there are others for whom it has become a title to be pursued by those longing to climb the corporate ladder. To have such recognition makes people feel powerful and significant in God. In the Bible, the apostle is the least of all, not the top of a spiritual pyramid. But it's not necessary to believe in apostles to learn from this prayer. Just consider what the term *apostle* meant in Jesus' day.

Jesus borrowed the concept of the word *apostle* from the Romans, who borrowed it from the Greeks. The Holy Spirit, who inspired the writing of Scripture, is quite practical, as it was this word that best described what Jesus was building in His Church on the earth— an apostolic movement. This Greek term describes the lead ship in an armada of ships. The responsibility of this great company of people was to recreate Roman culture in the newly conquered land by introducing Rome's educational system, language, arts, roads, and countless other values that had worked so well in Rome. The intention of this apostolic team was to create in this new land something so similar to Rome that if the Emperor were to visit, he would feel at home as much as he would in Rome. This helps us to understand the purpose of this prayer of Jesus much more clearly—*"on earth as it is in heaven."* He actually meant what He said. He's not trying to keep us busy with spiritual activities until one day He comes to rescue us from the prevailing darkness. He longs for places on the earth that remind Him of Heaven, places in which He feels at home. Prayer and radical obedience make such places possible.

This is the backbone of our commission. Everything we do—from raising healthy families, to preaching the Gospel and praying for the sick, to leading people to Christ—is all done to complete this very glorious assignment: Pray and obey until this world looks, thinks, and acts like His.

Church

We use the term *church* quite liberally. It describes the buildings we meet in. At times, we use it to describe the people we meet with. But this word is actually a secular term. And the Holy Spirit chose it above the many Hebrew and Aramaic terms available to describe what He was about to do. He could have chosen a Hebrew word. But He didn't. I personally believe He made this decision because the secular term was the only one that accurately described His intent.

The word for *church* is the Greek word *ekklesia*. This is the word the Holy Spirit used to describe His people on the earth. He used it when He said, *"I will build My church"* (Matt. 16:18). He could have used the word *temple, assembly,* or *tabernacle*. But He didn't because there is something very powerful and uniquely hidden in the word *ekklesia*, revealing a primary assignment. The origins of this word were not religious at all. Not even by implication. Ed Silvoso, in his masterpiece work entitled *Ekklesia: Rediscovering God's Instrument for Global Transformation*, defines *ekklesia* like this: "It had been used for centuries in both the Greek and Roman empires to refer to *a secular institution operating in the marketplace in a governmental capacity.*" That is stunning. It was secular in nature and was not used to describe religious gatherings.

Putting it another way, He was now going to plant His *ekklesia* within the surrounding systems of government and society in order to impregnate them with the DNA of the Kingdom of God. What's more, *ekklesia* could consist of a small handful of people. And together this small group represented the government of Heaven to bring about governmental influence here. This Greek and, eventually, Roman system was respected by the secular government themselves. Jesus doesn't rid us of the corporate concepts found in the word *temple* or *assembly* or *gathering.* Those terms reveal the stationary roles we have in our corporate meetings and smaller gatherings. This would well describe the meetings in the temple and from house to house (see Acts 5:42; 20:20). But *ekklesia* is different because it is mobile. It moves. It is wherever the people of God are. And they are governmental representatives, infusing the DNA of God's world into this one. Perhaps this is why Jesus emphasized, *"For where two or three have gathered together in My name, I am there in their midst"* (Matt. 18:20). The corporate gatherings are vital. But they are unto something. And that something is the governmental representation of the Kingdom of God found in the lives of two or three people in agreement, impacting the secular institutions in which they are planted.

Just the definition of this word is alarming. It's a gathering of two or three people, who exist in the marketplace, bringing governmental influence. What government? The Kingdom of God— His government.

Once again, I love our corporate gatherings. I think they are more important than most people realize. But the focus that Jesus had was not different. He wasn't destroying the need to gather. Instead He redefined who we are and what He has given us to do. Being consistent with our new nature we are to bring His government into this world's government by our presence in focused agreement. It is in this setting that we find the Kingdom of God has an effect on its surroundings like leaven does on a lump of dough (see Matt. 13:33).

It was this specific design that Jesus proclaimed would overpower the gates of Hades. It was this majority (two or three, with Jesus present) who would be able to displace the powers of darkness set against God's purposes in the earth. It was to this group of empowered representatives of His Kingdom that He said, *"I will give you the keys of the kingdom of heaven; and whatever you bind on earth shall have been bound in heaven, and whatever you loose on earth shall have been loosed in heaven"* (Matt. 16:19). We are now back to the model given in the Disciples' Prayer—*"on earth as it is in heaven."* Please notice, we don't bind on earth and then have it bound in Heaven. That's a poor translation, as you can't bind something in time and then have it bound in eternity. The New American Standard translation gets it right. We bind here what's already bound in Heaven. We loose here what's already loosed in Heaven. Ekklesia, wake up! We are governmental agents, representing another world, releasing the reality of that world into this one through agreement in purpose.

Paul

The most notable person in the New Testament besides Jesus Himself has to be the apostle Paul. His writings alone put him at least near the top of the list for the most influential people in the Bible. But what is sometimes forgotten, or even unknown to others, is that Paul's name was originally Saul. *Saul* is a nice Hebrew name. *Paul* is not. *Paul* is a very secular name that was given to him. Was it just to make his life more appealing to the secular audience he was speaking to? Why would God take His primary servant of the New Testament and give him a name that could be offensive to his Jewish audience? Especially when this Hebrew of Hebrews, this scholar of scholars, of the highest order of rabbis would be speaking into the international Jewish communities as well as to Gentiles?

While I may not be able to answer that question to either of our satisfaction, it is obvious that God is not offended by secular insinuations. He has a purpose, and much like He did with the words *apostle* and *church*, so He again will use whatever gives us the advantage to reveal His love to a group of people. He is, after all, the ultimate Father, who always loves well.

There were many name changes throughout Scripture. For example, Daniel's name was changed by the evil king he served. He became known as Belteshazzar, which was a Babylonian name. Daniel was also numbered among the witches and warlocks of his day, and at least initially not considered different from the others in his group. Being given a secular name in his assignment didn't seem to offend him, as in time the righteous stand out as what they do becomes noticeably different to everyone else around them. This was the case for Daniel, who became the highly favored one among the spiritual counselors to the king. He never would have had that place of influence if he had been offended at his name change. But even the change of Daniel's name was different from *Saul* to *Paul*.

Saul was renamed Paul, quite possibly by Sergius Paulus, for it happened after he and Barnabas ministered to this influential Roman citizen. It became a name of honor, as Paul now fully embraced his assignment to the Gentile world. It was at the point of this name change that this missionary pair was no longer recognized as Barnabas and Saul, but now Paul and Barnabas. The reversal in the order of mention was a sign of a positional upgrade for the one who is now called "Paul." This was an essential piece needed for Paul's own promotion into a role as a transformer of culture. A secular name cannot defile purpose or anointing. And in this case, the secular name would give credibility to those to whom God sent him to change and transform. He received the honor of a secular name to increase his impact on the Gentile world.

THE SOVEREIGNTY OF GOD

The sovereignty of God is one of the most beautiful things in existence. For me the picture of Jesus using secular words to reveal His Kingdom purposes is a wonderful look into that sovereignty. Did Jesus borrow from the Greeks and Romans? Yes, but that is only partially true. In the same way God used the nations who occupied the Promised Land to care for and steward the land before Israel took possession of it, so He allowed two great nations, the Greeks and Romans, to care for God-ideas of *apostle* and *ekklesia* before the time of His intended purpose. This is once again evidence to me that God loves and believes in the world around us, long before they deserve it or even believe it for themselves. In reality it is the same for all of us. That's why it's called grace. It would not be good for us, or for the world around us, if everything came from and through the Church. We need the privilege of recognizing and giving honor to the greatness that is outside of the Church. We need it. And so does the world.

SALT AND LIGHT

We can't add flavor to a world we're not a part of. Neither can we illuminate one room while we're in another. Our assignment by nature is to build ourselves up in our most holy faith, keep accountable, and go out by two or three to agree in prayer and bring change to every environment we touch. We are salt; we are light. This is *ekklesia*. This is us.

Those who are afraid of being defiled by the world have little faith in the power of the blood of Jesus that continually flows to keep us clean and the power of the Holy Spirit within us to guide, protect, and empower us to make a difference. This realization is a primary factor in our becoming transformational people.

We represent the government of Heaven every time we gather, even for coffee or to carpool to work. Two or three of us, with Jesus among us, are a majority in the world of influence. Now let's use the influence well.

Chapter Ten

THE POWER OF ASSUMPTIONS

What we assume about people affects our expectations of them and in turn influences how we treat them. It doesn't matter if it's a believer or a "pre-believer," our assumptions have extreme significance on what we give them of ourselves. If I misdiagnose who a person is and their place before God, I will mistreat them. In the natural we know that if a disease is mistreated, the problem is not cured, and sometimes an additional problem will occur as a result. Biblically based assumptions set a correct course that brings the best out of the people we love and serve. Heaven's culture is to influence our values so deeply that our perspective on people and their potential is to mirror the reality of that world.

PERSONAL LEARNING CURVE

In the early years of my walk with Jesus, I received strong discipleship training. There was a big emphasis on personal discipline, passion for Jesus, and giving everything to God. Absolute surrender was and is the only logical solution to finding our purpose in life in our walk with Christ. I am so grateful for this foundation. I long for those around me to realize the same focus and set of priorities. Such a background helped me to see things as black and white as they pertain to moral purity, ethics, and overall righteous living.

The hippie movement that said "anything goes" heavily influenced the culture of the day in my youth. In other words, rights and wrongs were negotiable according to how you wanted to live your life. They believed there were no absolutes. This was broadcast far and wide, eventually even by our educational systems. I remember so well hearing stories and examples designed to make one question whether or not there are absolutes in life. People seemed to spend considerable time imagining a situation in which cheating, lying, or immorality was okay. Because options listed by the storyteller never included God, the Bible as a resource, or prayer for a miracle breakthrough, it would seem that ethics and morality were fluid—ever changing.

This theology of the day was often called *situation ethics*, which basically means that circumstances determine what is right and wrong, moral and immoral, and there is no absolute moral code or compass. It was always entertaining to watch people create a make-believe set of circumstances that would make wrong things appear right and vice versa. It fascinates me to see people willing to work so hard to make their bad choices appear to be okay. If only that creative energy were used to create something of actual benefit for everyone.

In my early years of pastoring, another pastor and I decided to take a philosophy class at our local junior college. I don't remember why. I think we just wanted to step outside of our normal church environment and challenge our routine.

Our professor was a wonderful man who seemed to find unusual enjoyment when we had any kind of discussion over challenging subjects. He thrived on controversy, but not in an evil way. I never did figure out what he believed as he was so good at stirring up a good discussion in everyone else. I remember one day he had special joy when someone left a verse of Scripture on his desk before he arrived in class. It was the verse about not getting caught up in "empty philosophy." He didn't seem offended at all. It just gave him another chance to stir up conversation.

Christians don't always fare well in a setting of discussing controversial ideas. One of the reasons is that we tend to use Scripture to prove our point. It makes perfect sense to do so in our world. But it is usually a good indication of how out of touch we are to the world around us. It comes down to this: It rarely works if we're talking to people who have no value for the Bible. It makes the believer feel good because we're using Scripture. We sometimes even feel good about being rejected, which is a normal outcome in those situations. It qualifies as low-grade persecution to some. But we don't get any points when we suffer as a fool.

The Bible is God's Word. It carries the power of God for the complete transformation of a life, city, and nation. But it is not always the best use of truth to quote Scripture at people who have no value for it. I'm not saying God can't use it. I'd rather speak out of *biblical intelligence* (applying biblical principles without directly quoting the Bible), as this approach is extremely profitable in these conversations. The truth of His Word will often bear witness to what people know is true. His logic will outweigh anyone's brilliance when their beliefs contradict God's Word. In that context, we end up speaking from the absolutes of Scripture without requiring the hearer to believe in the Bible. The law of God is written in the heart, and speaking in this manner awakens such a God-given conviction to truth. That means the truth we speak of stands on its own, causing the hearer to rethink their values because of what we've said. Speaking out of biblical intelligence still carries the weight of the Word of God. And both His power and presence back it up. People then often become hungry for what the Bible has to say once they see your use of biblical principles for life.

One morning our philosophy class sat around tables of about eight people each. The room had several of these tables to accommodate all those present. It was to be a "lab" session, which meant we were to spend the entire class time discussing challenging subjects. The subject turned toward the issue of morality and absolutes. The young man across the table from me became extremely passionate in his efforts to convince the rest of us he was right. He raised his voice and declared, *"There are no absolutes!"* I asked him if he was *absolutely* sure, as his comment itself was an absolute. He just stared at me. He then went on to explain how *there is no right or wrong.* No sooner had these words come out of his mouth than someone from the group interrupted him in the middle of his heated discourse. He became very angry and said, "It's wrong for you to interrupt!" He hung himself with his own words. Such theories may look good on paper, but these theories won't stand the test of real life. He quickly discovered the foolishness of his comments, and his brilliant babble quickly dissipated.

The discipleship years were formative years for me. And I never want to depart from the important things I learned. I will always be a disciple. And yet there was a harshness that was somehow built into my thinking. Simply put, I believed other Christians didn't want to obey God and needed to be protected, persuaded, and controlled. The other side of that coin is the assumption that these believers would sin if I didn't help them. *They wanted to sin,* I thought. It sounds a little crazy when you say it out loud. I'm not even sure I would have agreed to that statement had I been asked that question in the day. But my actions said otherwise.

THE NEWSLETTER

I'll never forget reading part of a newsletter from another pastor. While I don't remember who it was, I can still see the newsletter— yellow paper, with a small column on the inside of the left page. He was writing to help other leaders. He stated that he realized that he had to make a change in how he viewed the people he was serving. Instead of assuming they wanted to sin, he now chose to treat them as though they wanted to do the right thing and obey God. In other words, he treated them as though he believed they were really saved. If he believed they were born again, he also had to believe that they had a new nature as a result. He went on to say that this approach had dramatic impact on what his people became. That hit me squarely between the eyes. I needed to hear this message that took only a few lines on the page of a newsletter.

It sounds strange to say that he now had to believe they were saved because why would anyone do anything else? Yet if you look at much of church ministry, it is aimed at keeping people from sin, instead of launching into their destiny in righteousness.

I quickly responded to the challenge that the pastor had given me in print. I had to change my assumptions about those around me to a more biblically-based assumption. It's so sobering to realize that we can live for years with a perception based on an understanding of the Word of God that was deficient and as a result be totally wrong. It was time to believe in their conversion. If they are truly born again, they have a new nature. And in that new nature is the desire to please God.

It's interesting that many pastors believe their people are born again yet still believe that the people would rather sin if they could get away with it. Perhaps we should take another look at what it means to be born again. When we are converted, the Holy Spirit takes up residence in us. Where? In our hearts—the absolute center of who we are. The journey to our conversion may cover many years, but the conversion itself is not gradual. It is in an instant. Maturity is a process, but not so with our conversion.

As believers, we are joined together with Christ in His death and resurrection. In that experience, our nature is changed. We are now saints, as the apostle Paul called us throughout his epistles.

It would be foolish to think that people lose their ability to sin. We don't. Adam and Eve sinned without a nature to do so. Our conversion, however, does change our ability to enjoy it. What does that mean? Our salvation has an inbuilt "bent" toward obeying God. Obeying God is now a part of our new nature. It doesn't mean we can no longer sin. It just means that it is not our nature to do so.

I changed my approach to the people in our church. Believing they want to obey God has a profound effect on what you teach and how you treat them when they're in crises or even if they have failed.

My time spent in counseling was also affected, as I would appeal to their heart of hearts that was set on obeying and honoring God. I remember even saying in one marriage counseling session, "I'm only meeting with you because I believe you are born again. And as those who are truly saved, you have a heart to do the right thing." We then looked at what was right for the circumstances they were facing in their marriage.

Few pastors seem to understand this, but we tend to get what we preach. Our pastoral and prophetic decrees have a greater impact on the reality that exists around us than we might have previously thought. That might explain why there is so much "backsliding" in churches who constantly speak about backsliding. When we speak to people about being confident of their identity in Christ, people are more prone to live from that place of faith and surrender.

ROMANS IDENTITY

In all Paul's letters written to churches, he called all believers saints. Imagine how different the book of Romans would have been if he had said, "To all the sinners in the church of Rome." We confess we are saved and are thankful for His forgiveness, but our self-image is often inconsistent with His work on our behalf. Our beliefs about ourselves often deny His work of redemption. His work on Calvary was so complete that He said, based on that reality, to "think of yourself as dead to sin." I think we have lessened the impact of this word by considering it to be an act of mere positive thinking. While positive thinking has a good effect on people's outlook on life, our nature is never changed through it. This teaching has got to be more than that. Otherwise, God is nothing more than a cheerleader trying to get our hopes up. Here's what the apostle Paul said: *"Knowing that Christ, having been raised from the dead, is never to die again...even so consider yourselves to be dead to sin, but alive to God in Christ Jesus"* (Rom. 6:9,11). There are many who will take a bullet in defending the death and resurrection of Christ, and rightly so. But these same individuals question their own new nature in Christ. When Paul says, *"even so consider yourself dead,"* he is revealing that in reality, our confidence in His death and resurrection and our new nature are to be one and the same. These two realities must be joined together as one thought, as that is how God sees it. My confidence in His death and resurrection is the basis for confidence in my personal transformation. The word *consider* basically implies "do the math." Add up the facts: *Jesus died + He was raised from the dead + our faith is in His redemptive work for our salvation = **we died with Him and have the nature of the resurrected Christ as our own.***

His work on our behalf must become the foundation for our new identity. And a good place to start in ensuring we have the right identity is to begin with our self-perception as free of sin, both in conduct and in intent.

It's hard to view others correctly if we don't see ourselves the way He does. Seeing ourselves correctly changes how we view other believers. Is it then not required of me to think of them in the same way He commanded me to think of myself? I believe so. This is what legitimizes the culture of honor in the family of God. We are not ignorant of the possibility of error or sin. That would be unhealthy and unreal. But to treat people as Christ sees them is wisdom. It is prophetically inspired wisdom.

THE REASONING BEHIND HONOR

When I consider the basis for the honor given to any individual, I look to the following three things: 1) We owe everyone honor because they were made in God's image; 2) We also owe each person honor because of the gifts and abilities that God gave them; 3) But for believers, there is an additional reason to give honor. It's because we recognize the Spirit of God in and upon their lives, and in doing so we celebrate their anointing and the call of God. This honor functions from a place of health and confidence in the work of Jesus on the cross and spills over by shaping a culture of value for people before they have earned it. Jesus did this to Peter. His name, Simon, meant "broken reed," but Jesus changed it to Peter, which means "rock." While he was still broken, Jesus called him *rock*.

TRUE IDENTITY HAS FRUIT

Believing in someone's conversion is a good beginning to serving people well. But this view of *who people are* significantly impacts our role as builders of His people and what we expect from them. I don't mean this in a heavy-handed, demanding way. As members of one another, we have the unique privilege of sowing into another person's destiny.

Every believer is a builder. It's not just pastors and leaders who carry this responsibility. That's why every member is exhorted to *build up* the Body of Christ. *"Therefore encourage one another and build up one another, just as you also are doing"* (1 Thess. 5:11). We are able to build with eternal effect through our understanding of God's Word on who He made us to be and what is now possible as sons and daughters of God.

All authority has two basic functions. It doesn't matter if it's the president of a nation, the CEO of a corporation, a pastor of a church, or the mom and dad of a household. Those two God-given responsibilities are to provide *protection* and, in the context of people's safety, bring *empowerment* for their purpose. Peter addressed this concept in First Peter 2:13-14:

> *Submit yourselves for the Lord's sake to every human institution...to governors as sent by him for the **punishment** of evildoers and the **praise** of those who do right.*

Punishment of evil protects society, while praise empowers its citizens into their God-given strengths. Punishment reinforces the boundaries needed for a healthy society, and praise celebrates those who make positive contribution to that healthy outcome.

FROM THE INDIVIDUAL TO THE WHOLE

As I begin to look at people the way Jesus does, forgiven and righteous before Him, I suddenly realize that my view of what is possible in my lifetime changes dramatically. That brings to us our view of the *last days*, which is called eschatology. There are many views and teachings about the last days, but for my taste all too few of them expect the Church to be victorious and glorious. In their view, sin usually increases until Jesus has to rescue His remnant. Seldom does righteousness increase in the earth according to their worldview. Darkness is on the rise, but seldom does light also increase. Isaiah 60:1-2 deals with this concept quite profoundly:

> *Arise, shine; for your light has come, and the glory of the Lord has risen upon you. For behold, darkness will cover the earth...but the Lord will rise upon you and His glory will appear upon you.*

Please note the context of increasing, rising light. It's when darkness increases. In other words, in the time of the enemy's greatest move, the Church answers with God's greatest move. There is no contest between light and darkness. Light always wins.

I don't want to lay out the theology for our hope in the glorious Church as much as the why. If I can believe that an individual is glorious and beautiful in their present state, then why can't I believe for the whole Church to live in this reality? And if I can believe for that, then why shouldn't I believe the world will respond to this, as the grace of God is irresistible? Believing in the beauty of honor given to people, anticipating the best about them, encouraging them for a glorious future, all have one obvious outcome: If I believe this about an individual, then I can no longer hold to the teaching that sin will get so bad that Jesus will have to come and rescue us to take us to Heaven. Sadly, that is a typical approach to eschatology, with so little faith in the power of the Gospel.

If I have hope for the individual, then I must nurture hope in my heart for the family, church, or city. I began to see that my confidence in the increase of sin in the earth was linked to inability to see how powerful this Gospel of salvation really was! Think about it—many believe in the power of darkness more than the power of the Gospel. Many have faith for the return of Christ, but not in the power of the good news of Jesus Christ to save the world from the very problems released by sin.

Confidence in the power of the Gospel is the offspring of this presence-based culture. It's hard to believe in darkness winning when the reality of Heaven permeates our values, attitudes, and ambitions. I'd like to suggest the anemic approach to the last days is often created in the absence of resurrection breakthroughs that this Gospel provides. And in that absence, being rescued makes a lot of sense.

We have the responsibility to establish righteous expectations of Jesus being exalted in all the earth. For then we will be positioned for more that we could have ever asked or imagined.

Chapter Eleven

FRIENDS BUILD WITH ETERNITY IN MIND

One of the strongest ways of illustrating and releasing the culture of His world into ours is by how we do relationships. Jesus said they will know of our faith in Christ by our love for each other. Listen to those words: *They will know.* One of the most profound tools of evangelism ever is this simple truth. Love each other well. Not only does it bring strength to one another and glorify God, it draws people to Christ. Could it be any clearer? I don't think so. The impact we are to have on revealing the culture of Heaven is in part by how we love and serve each other.

Relationships done well also attract the presence of God. He said He would be with the two or three gathered in His name. In attracting His presence, we automatically attract the reality of His world into our environment. They are inseparable. This is, in part, a fulfillment of the commission we have to see His Kingdom come.

A wonderful African proverb comes to mind in light of this subject: "If you want to go fast, go alone. But if you want to far, go together." That is so true. It is common to see short spurts of success and breakthrough throughout the Church. These successes are often accomplished by individuals who have good hearts, great faith, and exciting zeal. But the breakthroughs often don't last, because there is no community on board to sustain them. They went fast, but they weren't able to go far. Our successes in life, in many ways, depend on community. People loving people. My approach is this: *If the vision for my life doesn't require the help of others, it's too small of a vision.*

All Kingdom realities are realized and sustained through family. The Scripture says, *"Our **Father**...for yours is the **kingdom**"* (Matt. 6:9-13). Any time we leave the concept of family, we've left the subject of Kingdom. The family of God is His target, and that family is community. And by implication, they are in fellowship with one another, which is communing. Fellowship is the exchange of life, one member to another. We need each other to become all that God intended.

The reality is that we cannot get to where God wants us to go on our own. Sometimes He will not even speak to us about a matter. It's not punishment. God is not giving us the cold shoulder or the silent treatment. Sometimes He wants us to rediscover what He has already spoken to us. But then there are times when we are to learn to receive from another member of the Body of Christ. He is emphasizing that we are members of one body. Consider David, who wanted to build a temple for God. In Acts 2 David is called a prophet, so that only adds to our understanding that he hears from God brilliantly. But God wouldn't give him any direction for this dream that was in his heart. So he turned his heart toward the gift that God had given him in a man. This partnership in life and ministry was found in the prophet Nathan. This wonderful prophet was able to give David the word that he was looking for. And while it wasn't what he wanted, it was what he preferred—the will of God.

ROADBLOCKS AND FREEWAYS

It is also true that other people can slow down your progress and growth. Joining with the wrong people can inhibit growth and progress, not increase it. There are those who are so driven by their own agenda for life that they can't hear or give time to another person's purpose in life. Bless them and love them. But don't waste your time developing a one-sided relationship without a clear word from God.

I've tried to make it a practice to serve everyone in front of me, regardless of whether they seem to be for me or against me. But I only pour my time into those who have that *fire in their eyes* when I declare our purpose in life. These are the ones whose hearts become passionate over the word that I carry.

Obviously, my role as a pastor is different from that of most people who read this book. But the principles are applicable to any environment. Simply put, find those whose hearts burn for Jesus like your heart. Connect with those who are humble, loving, and servant-hearted. And the more you discover loyalty in them, strengthen the relationship. As you do this, learn to do life together.

It's in accountability that we find some of our greatest strength. Live with friends to whom we can give an account for how we are managing our strengths and weaknesses. Accountability is usually thought of as the way we help one another with sins and weaknesses that we may struggle with. And that is true. But it's only part of the story. Accountability needs to become holding each other accountable for fulfilling our dreams and purposes in life. Accountability—give an *account* for our *ability*. Loyal friends are treasures.

By the way, loyalty for one person or group is never to be proven by rejecting another. That is worldly loyalty, not Kingdom. In the Kingdom we love all, but are wise enough to recognize our family and our tribe.

DECADES WELL SPENT

I pastored for 17 years in Weaverville, California. And now I've pastored in Redding, California for 22 years. The idea of long-term commitment is very appealing to me, as I believe it is in the heart of the Father. My senior associate, Kris Vallotton, and I have been together for 39 years. Dann Farrelly, a centerpiece in our senior leadership team, was at Bethel before I got here and has been with me for 22 years. Charlie Harper was on the leadership team in Weaverville and has come to Redding to help. He's another one who has served faithfully for nearly 40 years. My children, Eric, Brian, and Leah, have been on board in this movement all their lives but have been in staff positions for around 20 years. We have elders who have served for many decades. In fact, most of our amazing team has been here for many, many years, serving faithfully. This list could go on and on. What has been discovered is that when we serve together, it is possible to have greater impact as the number *two* person than a person would have if they were number *one* in another environment.

The point of all this is that many of these individuals could go anywhere and accomplish much for the Kingdom, establishing their own ministries. And no one would fault them. We know there are times when that is the heart of God for an individual, and we honor and celebrate that move. But many on our team have chosen to stay here, in relationship, living out their dream in the context of an empowering community. In many environments sons have to leave to become fathers elsewhere. Healthy environments give place to become fathers at home.

It is the heart of God to have a group of people discover what could be accomplished through the sometimes-painful process of doing life together with other empowered people. There are conflicts. There is pain. And there are great letdowns and disappointments. But there is also honor, growth, breakthrough, and unexpected blessings.

We really do want to go far and, in doing so, leave something for the next generation.

LEARNING FROM POWER

From what I understand, the atomic bomb was made through the principle of *fission*. That is where an atom is split, releasing an amazing amount of power. We know the reality of this fact through the bombs that were dropped in World War II. But there is a superior power that is made through the concept of *fusion*. That is where two atoms are merged together. And in doing so, there is a release of *seven times* the amount of power than there is through the splitting of an atom. Uniting is exponentially more powerful than dividing. This is a profound truth that applies to all of us. Churches split, and there's a release of new vision and power. What would happen if these churches would unite?

Obviously, unity in the church is big in God's heart. And this concept is very useful in that setting. But I'm talking about unity that is a bit different, perhaps a bit more mature. Unity begins with simple things like respecting one another and giving honor or value to one another. That's a good beginning. But God is looking for people who will actually get to know each other and give their lives for one another. Partnerships in life are essential. Longevity is essential. That's where we learn to help to partner with each other's dreams.

DREAMS ARE DESIGNED TO BE FULFILLED

Consider this—both Pharaoh and Joseph had dreams (see Gen. 37:5; 41:1). They had great destinies and God-given purpose. But neither could reach the fulfillment of their dream without the other. It wasn't until Joseph served the dream of an ungodly king that God fulfilled his own. This is amazing. It's a unique call to serve the dream of another. It's what friends, family, and partners do. For when one of us gets a breakthrough, it causes a domino effect for the rest of us. One person's victory is the victory of us all. Thinking like members of a body will help give us perspective on how this Kingdom works and how it can be successfully released into our churches and communities.

One of my greatest privileges in life is to have covenant friendships with a number of people. This is practiced and appreciated daily with the Bethel staff. But the Lord also called six couples together to form an alliance. This happened around ten years ago. They are John and Carol Arnott, Randy and DeAnne Clark, Che and Sue Ahn, Georgian and Winnie Banov, Rolland and Heidi Baker, and Beni and me. We formed a group that we call Revival Alliance. We have learned that through friendship and partnership in ministry, we would be able to accomplish far more serving each other than we ever could fighting on our own.

Each leader has his or her own network of churches and leaders. Combined together, this would amount to tens of thousands of churches and even more leaders. Some would think it's a perfect setting to form one new denomination. But we chose not to do that. We specifically wanted to be united in our diversity rather than to create uniformity. It was in our hearts to illustrate how different groups can sow into the others to help them be successful. I often speak to the leaders of these various groups, serving their unique vision and working to make them successful in life. No one is ever concerned that one in this group will try to steal members so they have a bigger roster of members. It would never even enter our minds. The point is we have found pleasure in serving another person's dream. But we don't keep this principle only for each other. We each serve the wider Body of Christ, enjoying the privilege of loving, speaking into, and learning from other streams in the Body of Christ. What a great privilege, as none of us has all there is to have for these last days. We need each other. The fact that we could partner with others we'd normally not have access to has been a great eye-opener for me. So many rich wonders of the Gospel are found in other groups. I am so thankful for the privilege of cross-pollinating.

AM I A FATHER OR A BROTHER?

Fathers and brothers act completely differently as it pertains to success in the family. Brothers often get jealous of another person's success. We've noticed that fairly often spiritual leaders live like brothers and try to keep potentially big people small, just so that no one surpasses them in significance. It's called jealousy, and it is the Saul/David story all over again—*"Saul has killed his thousands. David has killed his ten thousands"* (see 1 Sam. 18:7). This is weakness. Healthy fathers want their sons and daughters to surpass them in every way. They celebrate their successes while brothers mock, resist, or try to discredit one who surpasses them.

GOD'S HEART OF PLEASURE FOR PEOPLE

I was looking through *Charisma Magazine* a while back and took special note of all the different conferences being advertised. This is a huge part of our ministry, so I have appreciation for these events. People sacrifice so much to be a part only to learn how to represent Jesus better and, in turn, bring a more powerful impact on the world around them.

I noticed that I winced somewhat at the names and pictures of some of the speakers, which revealed something in my heart that wasn't good. I had no reason to distrust them, but I also didn't trust them. I knew enough not to criticize or reject them. But my response did disappoint me.

I thought I'd try something that I practice often in other settings. One at a time, I would find whatever person I questioned and look at their picture until I felt the pleasure of the Lord for them. His pleasure for people is usually experienced in my heart as compassion and honor for them. It comes up from the very center of my being, where the Holy Spirit lives. It's very hard to be angry with a person, or jealous, or even distrustful when you feel God's pleasure over another person. In fact, feeling the pleasure of the Lord for people is a sure antidote for jealousy. This changed everything. This principle has had a powerful impact on the way I deal with people, both good and bad. Sensing God's heart for others keeps us from a typical religious response and brings us into a connection with His love for people.

ETERNITY STARTS NOW

What we are talking about is the value system of Heaven for the people of this world. Managing our relationships for the glory of God reveals an aspect of His nature to the world around us that they can get no other way. Meaningful relationships take time and are expensive in the sense of investment of emotional energy. But the dividends are eternal. So it starts now.

Chapter Twelve

A "PERMISSIONAL" CULTURE

Jesus was capable of addressing the secrets of the heart in ways that are almost unknown today. It may be my imagination, but it appears to me that people were thankful when Jesus confronted them. His words were so life-giving. Even when Jesus spoke of things they didn't understand, those words brought them life—if, of course, they listened with their hearts. That is exactly what happened when Jesus gave His most offensive sermon of all—*"eat My flesh and drink My blood"* (see John 6). At the end of the message, after a mass exodus by the crowd of thousands, Jesus asked His disciples if they were also going. Peter responded, *"Lord, to whom shall we go? You have the words of eternal life"* (John 6:68 NKJV). To me Peter was saying, "We don't understand Your message about eating Your flesh or drinking Your blood any more than the crowd that left. But what we do know is that whenever You speak, we come alive inside."

Jesus modeled the ultimate culture of confrontation. That culture was matched and surpassed by the honor He gave to those around

Him. Jesus was known for trusting people long before they deserved it. The examples are so many that it would be rather tiring to list them all. But one very notable example is with the demoniac referred to as the man of the Gadarenes (see Matt. 8:28-34). This man had so many demons that when Jesus cast them out into the pigs, 2,000 pigs committed suicide by drowning in the sea. That is a significant amount of torment. For me, the most amazing part of the story is that when this newly delivered man wanted to follow Jesus, He said no. In my mind, if anyone needed a little extra help and training before being sent home, it was this man. Instead, Jesus sent him back to his hometown to testify of what God had done for him. That's a lot of responsibility given to a newly delivered man, especially when you consider that he had no one else of like mind in his hometown. The city had driven Jesus and the disciples from their region (see Matt. 8:34).

You can tell how much God trusts you by considering what He has entrusted to you. In this case, the destinies of the cities in this region were placed under the responsibility of a man who had just been set free. How long has this man been delivered? An hour? Two? Long enough to put on clothes, which tells us in part the measure of his torment (see Mark 5:15). The point is, this man wouldn't be allowed to pick up trash in the church parking lot in many churches around our nation. And he certainly wouldn't be allowed to preach. But Jesus sent him to his hometown as the only evangelist for the region. We tend to overtrain, to compensate for our own lack of faith in a person's conversion. This story reveals the greatest risk in ministry I can find. The reward for this risk was the next time Jesus came back to that region, every person from every city showed up to hear Him speak. The cities that drove Jesus out of town couldn't wait for the privilege of hearing Him again. This is quite a difference. It is the remarkable impact of one untrained man to awaken an entire region to the purposes of God. And it worked.

As powerful as the example of the man of the Gadarenes is, it's Jesus' trust in His disciples that astonishes me most. These were men whom He spent time with, only to discover, day after day, how completely unqualified they were for the profound and powerful ministry Jesus had in mind. But when you realize what qualifies a person to Jesus, you see they were perfectly chosen and qualified. And so are we.

CULTURAL SHIFT

To say Jesus inspires me sounds like a silly understatement. Yet it's true. More specifically, it's His unusual way of training people that surprises me and yet provokes me to the lifestyle of risk that was His norm. And I want to challenge what we typically think when we think of His training methods.

Jesus sent His 12 disciples back to their hometowns for ministry. They went in pairs, bringing back to Him the stories of the breakthroughs they had only seen through Jesus' hands. And now it happened through their own. To say they were excited was yet another understatement. It moved Jesus enough to take them away for some rest. What happened is quite predictable, but Jesus' response was the surprise.

> An argument started among them as to which of them might be the greatest. But Jesus, knowing what they were thinking in their heart, took a child and stood him by His side, and said to them, "Whoever receives this child in My name receives Me, and whoever receives Me receives Him who sent Me; for the one who is least among all of you, this is the one who is great" (Luke 9:46-48).

Success in ministry brings things to the surface in us that problems and difficulties will never cause to rise. Such is the case in this story. It was only after Jesus gave them power and authority over demons and disease that they argued about being great. It was their success. Their breakthroughs. I'm sure they thought the supernatural manifestations of God in their own hometowns surpassed those of any of the rest of the guys. For this reason, they argued for their own greatness. And what moves me so deeply is that Jesus never rebuked them for thinking themselves great. Everyone who spent time with Jesus began to dream of significance. And yet it was their understanding of greatness that was in error. Not the desire. Jesus pruned their understanding back to His perspective. The least is the greatest. The servant of all is the greatest. The child is the greatest. They got it.

The *who is great* debate was finished, but there were more issues that were about to arise in their hearts because of their success. John, thinking he did something good, told Jesus how he dealt with those who were casting out demons in Jesus' name but were not a part of the twelve.

> *John answered and said, "Master, we saw someone casting*
> *out demons in Your name; and we tried to prevent him*
> *because he does not follow along with us"* (Luke 9:49).

For me it's like John, referring to a group separate from the 12 disciples, is saying, "Okay, we know that we're not better than each other. But certainly, we are greater than they are." They had been learning the issue of loyalty and devotion to the team. But in the Kingdom, loyalty to one never requires disloyalty to another. It's not a competition against one another. It's a race against time. Jesus was happy to hear of people being freed through His name. And He no doubt rejoiced over the fact that people who were not a part of the *inside 12* were committing themselves to His passion. Jesus pruned back their understanding of loyalty to a place that would grow fruit for the Kingdom when He said, *"Do not hinder him; for he who is not against you is for you"* (Luke 9:50).

This was a new way to look at people. It would have been much more common to think that those who are not for you are against you. But this was a significant shift in their thinking of others. This insight would help most of us as we deal with leaders of business, politics, education, etc.

Even though this must have been a painful lesson, there was one more issue that was to surface before the *post-ministry success lessons* were over. This third and final problem was the most serious by far.

Jesus sent messengers ahead of Him to prepare provisions for Him and His disciples in a city of the Samaritans. The city refused. James and John were outraged, and offered to call down fire on them all.

> When His disciples James and John saw this, they said, "Lord, do You want us to command fire to come down from heaven and consume them?" (Luke 9:54).

It is very easy to think we're moving in righteous anger when in fact we're reacting to the pain of rejection. Maturity knows the difference. What kind of meetings must they have had in their hometowns to make them think this was actually possible if Jesus merely gave the nod of approval?

Some translations add to their request, *"As Elijah did."* They're not the first to use Scriptures to support their wrong behavior.

Let's be honest. Moving in the *spirit of murder* is a serious offense. And Jesus didn't treat it lightly, but followed their request with a stern rebuke and once again pruned their misconception of the Kingdom. Before we look at Jesus' response, let's look at what He didn't do. He didn't punish His team. He didn't set them on the sidelines of ministry for a season until they learned the proper treatment of those who disagree. I don't even want to imply that those kinds of responses don't have merit in certain situations. But for most of us, this situation was grounds enough for at least a *time out*. Instead, Jesus refined their perception of how His Kingdom works.

> But He turned and rebuked them, [and said, "You do not know what kind of spirit you are of; for the Son of Man

did not come to destroy men's lives, but to save them"]
(Luke 9:55-56).

That's an amazing rebuke, if in fact they used Elijah as an example to justify their actions. What was done by Elijah was by the Spirit of God. What they wanted to do, similar to Elijah, was of a different spirit. The implication is an evil spirit. Same action, different spirit. The clarifying thought came when Jesus redefined for them why He came to earth. It wasn't to destroy men's lives. It was to save them. I wish more ministries would embrace this mandate instead of continually trying to do as Elijah did.

SUCCESSFUL BY GOD'S STANDARDS

If we were to look at the journey of the disciples in their ministry experience as recorded in Luke 9, I think most of us would admit this was a risky and costly endeavor. And while Jesus corrected them over every issue of the heart that surfaced following their successful ministry trip, He also empowered them. He didn't just point out what was wrong. He gave them His perspective in every issue of the heart. But what is the most astonishing of all that transpired in this journey is what followed. I remind you, there are no chapter divisions in the original text.

> *Now after this the Lord appointed seventy others, and sent them in pairs ahead of Him to every city and place where He Himself was going to come* (Luke 10:1).

That actually sounds funny to me. What many leaders would have called a failure—empowering unqualified disciples for ministry only to have them follow their success with arrogance, elitism, and the spirit of murder—and then following that by appointing 70 others to the same task is exactly what Jesus did. It should become apparent that Jesus is not quite as nervous about messes as most of us are. He expanded the teams that would be doing what the 12 did so that more people could be touched, with obvious implications that the messes could also increase.

Instead of reading into the story that God doesn't care about mistakes or deep issues of flawed character, look at what moves Him—co-laborers who work to represent Him well by bringing freedom to captives and healing to those in need. Also worth noting is that in each case, Jesus pruned their thinking by redefining values and concepts. All pruning is done by His voice for more fruitfulness (see John 15:2-3). Pruning by nature acknowledges fruitfulness but brings adjustments for the purpose of greater increase.

A HARD LESSON LEARNED

Many years ago, I had a leader who failed badly. It wasn't moral. But it was serious. I removed him from all ministry for a season. To this day, I know there are times when this must be done. But in our situation, I had the Lord speak to me clearly about my decision through this verse: *"Then the Spirit of the Lord will come upon you mightily, and you shall prophesy with them and be changed into another man"* (1 Sam. 10:6).

What I believe the Lord showed me was that if I kept this leader from the anointing of God he would experience in ministry, I would be keeping him from the very thing that would turn him into another man. I realize that in the scripture above, Saul did not remain devoted to the Lord. But that is not the fault of the experience. He didn't steward the grace that God gave him in that moment and forfeited the momentum that God created for his personal victory. The truth remains—the anointing of God upon us makes personal transformation much more available.

I met with this man and explained the change I wanted to make in his responsibilities and why. He embraced it and moved out of that failure into great purity, success, and reputable ministry.

OUR ATTEMPT AT DISCIPLESHIP

I have tried for years to create an atmosphere where people can dream and become all God intended. I have no ownership of people or their gifts. If they are a part of our team, then I must be certain they really have my heart before I entrust them with great authority. But this is the journey we've been on for as long as I can remember.

We have what I call a *"permissional" culture.* This is where people are given permission and empowered to dream and experiment with how to fulfill their purpose and accomplish their assignment in life. Once a team member has my dream deep in their hearts, I want them to dream on their own. Because then I know their dream will not cause *division* but instead will enhance our overall purpose. For this reason, I empower my team with few restrictions. I do this for those who have proven themselves as faithful, but oftentimes even to those who don't deserve it. Sometimes they do make a big mess. I can't say that is fun, but it is necessary. Jesus didn't seem to be afraid of the consequences of empowering His disciples.

I have found that it is worth the risk to empower people, for in doing so they often rise to heights way beyond any of our expectations. Some people just need someone to believe in them in order to grow into their potential. It is worth the risk. And messes can be cleaned up. This cultural perspective can also be applied to business or even the home.

Here are some helpful principles to follow:

1. Believe in people before they earn it. Jesus set the standard quite high for us as He entrusted the good news of the Kingdom of God long before they could ever earn the right to it.

2. Give people the benefit of the doubt. Be honest, confront, but also believe the best about them until proven

otherwise. And if proven otherwise, give them room to grow and change by believing in their repentance.

3. Discipline according to what's best for them, not for what makes you look good. Correction is not to make us feel better or vindicated. It must be entirely for others, with a hope for their future.

4. Give responsibility liberally, authority sparingly. I give responsibility to willing people. But I will only give authority to the tested and proven. The biggest mistake I made in ministry was giving authority to someone too early. It was costly.

TRAINING FOR ETERNITY

Let's face it. Jesus trained people differently than we do, and differently than what makes us comfortable. But once again, it is we who need to change.

There is much at stake. Our ways are not better than His. He took risks with people that many of us never would have taken.

For many years now, we've tried to follow His example, with both glorious and disastrous results. It is probably true that some of the disasters could have been avoided or lessened with greater wisdom. But one thing is for sure—we've had some glorious outcomes that never would have happened if we did not believe in and empower people who did not deserve it. The results are clear—more people healed, saved, and delivered; more passion for Jesus, and a profound devotion to one another; and a higher standard of personal purity with great devotion to Jesus. We will continue to learn how to bring forth the fruit that He deserves.

Chapter Thirteen

UNIQUE EXPRESSIONS
OF WORSHIP

O ne of the most frequent questions I'm asked is, "How do you balance between ministry and family?" It is a great question that plagues most households in the faith, as we long to be faithful in ministry, the home, work, and involvement in our communities. Juggling the everyday affairs of life and managing a healthy home environment is a challenging task, for sure. But to be completely honest, I don't like the word "balance." Of late it's become a term used to describe mediocrity—that place between joy and depression. Yet I always try to answer through what I've learned in my own journey.

When I was young in the faith, there was a whole group of leaders in the church who were learning the importance of family. It almost sounds funny to say, but it's true. Many in prior generations had sacrificed their families as the price they felt God wanted them to pay for the ministry God had called them to. It was sincere, and often taught in the Bible schools of their day. The results were nothing short of tragic. This new emphasis on family was refreshing, becoming what many needed to hear. It gave them permission to prioritize their families in a way that was already in their hearts. This emphasis was so encouraging to me as a newly married man. It gave me hope for the church to hear that many leaders were now declaring the importance of our own homes in a way that my parents taught us.

I remember attending pastors' conferences in which lists of priorities were made to help us learn what was important to God. God was always first. Family was second. Then our call or ministry was next, followed by our devotion to the church itself. It went from there to occupations, hobbies, and the like. While some would differ in parts of the order I listed, the main point I want to identify is that God is logically number one, followed by our families, etc.

NUMBER ONE

As I began to pastor Mountain Chapel in Weaverville, California, the Lord started challenging me about my priorities in ways that were a great surprise. My discovery was quite astonishing to me and started me on a journey that affected my life in ways far beyond the obvious application of God and my family as priorities. My discovery was almost what some would call a rude awakening. It was this: *When God is number one, there is no number two.*

So much of my prayer time and my study time was built around my family. What I mean by that is that they were the focus of most of my prayers, and my study was on how to be a good dad and husband. It's not that I didn't pray for the church or our city. I did. A lot. But it was family that captured my heart in ways that are tough to describe. I prayed for my children and their spouses while they were still infants. I searched the Scriptures for promises about my children and what they would accomplish in their lifetime. I memorized some of those verses or would read them out loud when in prayer. I declared them into our sanctuary as I'd walk and pray during the week. My prayer times in our home were captured by this one purpose—that my children would love God and serve Him joyfully. That was it. I felt I could die a happy man if I was able to see that one dream fulfilled.

And yet my heart burned for God in ways hard to describe. I wanted only to please Him. People's opinions of me, my family, or even the church mattered very little to me. I simply wanted to know that I had fulfilled my purpose in life and had done so in a way that was pleasing to the Lord in every area of my life.

So now I was given an unusual mandate that I had never heard anyone teach on or explain: *When God is number one, there is no number two.* This would end up changing most every area of my life, as it reveals God's approach to our lives in ways that the wonderful list of priorities never could.

THERE IS NO NUMBER TWO

I honestly felt that I heard the Lord speak that phrase to me—*When God is number one, there is no number two.* It started to make sense to me that as long as I had a list of priorities, I'd have to leave my first priority to do the second, and so on. This new insight implied I could only serve God. I guess that's logical. But the implications were life-changing, as I had to learn how those things could become a part of my service to God. All of those things were to be an offering to Him.

Every area of my life must be part of my worship of God Himself. If there's a part of my life that cannot be an expression of my love for God, it shouldn't be in my life.

This change in perspective didn't change my practice as much as it changed my confidence that I was delighting God's heart. I always made family first. But what I didn't realize was how much God was being loved through my love for my wife and children. There is no vacation from God. I don't stop my service to God while I serve people. It's actually quite the opposite. He takes it personally. Something happens when you realize that what you're doing brings pleasure to His heart. Our personal esteem and confidence grow dramatically.

ONLY THE BEGINNING

This started me on a journey where I discovered things in the Scriptures I hadn't noticed as deeply before. For example, when Jesus taught about our visiting the person in prison or giving a cup of cold water to someone He said, *"When you've done it to the least of these, you've done it unto Me"* (see Matt. 25:40). There's not one of us who would not be ecstatic beyond reason for the privilege of giving Jesus a cup of water. And yet when we serve and love people, He takes it personally. It's as though He is in the room and it was Him we served. It seems to me that if we better understand His delight in the things we do for others, our awareness of His heart will grow exponentially. It is possible to serve people and not really love God. That's the whole point of 1 Corinthians 13. But it's impossible to really love God and not love and serve people. And the beauty is, we don't honor people separate from God but instead *unto God.*

We stand in God's presence, sometimes by the hour, honoring God with our thanksgiving and praise, responding to Him deeply in worship. It is a privilege beyond measure that we are invited into God's throne room to minister to Him. It is in this hallowed place that we tell Him how much we love Him. That is correctly called worship. But He is the one who broadens the subject by suggesting that any time we do an act of kindness to another person, He receives it as unto Himself. Realizing this helps me to see that God wants me to do all that I do *as unto the Lord* and *with all of my might,* He calls it worship.

I knew that worship was more than the songs we sing to Him on a Sunday morning service, but little did I know that visiting someone in prison was worship. Little did I know that caring for the simplest of needs of my family is something He values as worship. A few years ago I was told that Jews considered work to be one of their expressions of worship. This idea added much clarity to my thinking.

A NEW UNDERSTANDING

This new insight changed so many things for me. It helped me to see that every part of life is beautiful and has the potential to bring Him glory. Merely offering our efforts unto Him sanctifies that which was previously thought to be secular, vain, or mundane. I was able to see that every part of my life was sanctified by its eternal purpose.

So many think ministry is standing behind a pulpit and preaching. Thankfully that is included, as that is a part of my assignment. But in reality it is a very small part of that vast subject. This is important to understand. If we don't realize what our actions mean to God, we do not receive the strength and encouragement God intended for us out of our own obedience.

The moment all of us are waiting for is when He says, *"Well done, good and faithful servant"* (Matt. 25:23). I realize this is speaking of a future event. But He breathes that into our heart every time we know with confidence that we have done the will of God. Doing what brings Him pleasure, whether it's preaching, praying for the sick, or going on a picnic with my family, delights the heart of our Father who takes it personally. It's the manner in which we do what we do. Laying hands on the sick, or working in the garden, or even going to a Little League game all become spiritual activities because of who they are done for. Worship sanctifies the offering.

One of the priorities of my financial life has been to give to missions—the ministry of the Gospel around the world. I learned this as a young man and embraced it as one of the great privileges for my life. Beni and I shared our passion with others to encourage them to do the same, but never made our giving amounts or percentages known. It has always been important for us to keep that private. Whenever you sow money sacrificially, there's a sense of personal reward for responding to the opportunity to give with eternity in mind. This was especially true when our giving cost us personal comfort or fulfillment of dreams. I don't think there are many who would read this who wouldn't agree that this kind of giving is spiritual. But here was my challenge. While I never neglected my wife and children, I never had the same sense of spiritual achievement when I spent money to meet their needs and desires. Don't misunderstand me—it was always a joy and privilege. I just never considered it to be spiritual. But it was. I realized that spending money to meet my family's needs or helping the missionary to meet their family's needs are both intensely spiritual from our Father's perspective. This shift in thinking helped me to enjoy every decision, benefiting from the knowledge that I had just done the will of God.

Obedience is one of the ways He gives strength to His people. Jesus put it this way: *"My food is to do the will of Him who sent Me and to accomplish His work"* (John 4:34). The will of God nourishes the soul in the same way that healthy food nourishes the body bringing it great strength. If we are ignorant of what brings Him joy, we live unconscious of the strength and encouragement that He made available for us in the action. Obeying Him releases strength and confidence to us, but it also helps to establish our identity in Christ. These are true spiritual nutrients.

Living conscious of His delight in the simple things in life is key to a godly self-esteem. In turn we are able to live in the strength intended from eating this heavenly meal called *obedience*. This could be misunderstood as performance for favor. It's not. This is the act of worship that comes from the favor we already have received. Healthy self-perception is the fruit.

Obedience is key in our understanding and affirming our identity. Jesus said, *"No longer do I call you slaves, for the slave does not know what his master is doing; but **I have called you friends**, for all things that I have heard from My Father I have made known to you"* (John 15:15). Having an identity as a friend of God has tremendous impact on our spiritual self-esteem, as it should. But what preceded this statement was what gave us access to that friendship. *"You are My friends **if you do what I command** you"* (John 15:14). Obedience makes becoming a friend of God even possible. It is also how we prove our love for Him. *"If you love Me, you will keep My commandments"* (John 14:15).

If we don't know that caring for the poor or praying for the sick and tormented can be a part of our worship expression, we fail to draw upon our identity as friends of God called to change the world. Also, if we don't understand that going on a vacation with our family or watching our children and grandchildren in their sporting or musical activities is a part of our worship expression, we live below what God intended for us. We miss out on perceiving the face of a Father who delights in us, which is the great reward of this change in perspective.

When we stand before the Lord, we will watch as He honors those who have led millions to Christ or have served in a foreign land bringing the good news to people who otherwise never would have heard the Gospel. But we will also see Him give a high place of honor to the couple who spent the bulk of their adult life caring for a handicapped child, or to those who over and over visited their parents or grandparents with Alzheimer's, who never once remembered their previous visit. Things look different from His perspective. Only He can clearly see the beauty of a cup of water given in His name. Only He sees the heart of worship from the simplest of activities. And He rewards accordingly.

WHOLENESS IN LIFE

For a culture to influence entire cities and then nations, it has to exhibit health in all aspects of life—family, work, play, rest, etc. Where we truly succeed, people will long for the same. Practical Kingdom success attracts the masses. Picture a city set on a hill that is all lit up, and it's nighttime. Those who need shelter rejoice when they see the city that is so prominent in the landscape. They know exactly where to go. When we have excellence and success in these areas, we have an impact on the world around us.

Children probably learn more through play than in any other time of life. This is where they learn that learning is fun and that taking risks is a part of life. They are driven to climb higher, run faster, and yell the loudest. Riding bikes is fun. But seldom do they leave it at that. They try to ride up ramps and sail through the air. They lift the front wheel off the ground and see how long they ride on the back wheel. It is all a part of play. It is all a part of learning.

Laughter is a huge part of play, which distinguishes them from their adult counterparts. This should concern us, as Jesus said we are to become like children. Learning to enjoy life and celebrate every part is so liberating. It actually releases us into our destiny and purpose.

CULTURE IS FORMED AT HOME

Culture is first experienced and designed in the home. For those who are single, it's in the relationships with other singles and families. The point is, it is formed in miniature before it is transformational. We learned in time what was most important for us in raising our children. And while these lifestyle choices were for our family, they are applicable for every believer and even transferrable to a local church. We intentionally exposed our children to the following:

Compassion

For many years, we lived on a main street, behind the church facilities. Many people in need would come to our doors asking for help. Sometimes they would need a place to sleep for the night. Many times, we brought people in just to love and serve them while they were passing through our community of Weaverville. There is a danger element whenever you bring a stranger into your home, which meant we really had to pray for discernment on whom to welcome. Safety for my family is priority number one. We served people to show the love of Christ. But the benefit was that we were able to train our children in having compassion for others and what to do about it. We even had a young couple live with us for a season after they had received Christ but were living in their camper. We also had a number of foster children live with us through the years. Their backgrounds were horrific. Opportunities to show compassion are everywhere. We must be intentional, as we tend to insulate ourselves from human need.

World Need

We would take our children to an orphanage in Mexico just about every year. We'd help with their building projects and help in their outreaches. One of the most moving ministries was for the people who lived at the dump. They tried to scratch out a living with throw-away items and ate very undesirable food. Our teams, including my children, would bring food, blankets, and clothing. The experience of facing such horrible poverty and then doing something about it is a thousand times better than telling them we need to care for people in other nations. It is said that 95 percent of the money that comes into the American Church is spent on itself. Exposure to world need could change that percentage dramatically. I know it has for me.

Generosity

This is one of my core values for my life. I learned it early on as a child. Raising my children in that environment is one of the most important things I can give them. (The same is true with the church I pastor.) Generosity is usually applied to money. But it is also about giving time, words, acts of kindness, and the like to simply reveal what the Father is like. Teaching children about this part of life is critical.

Holy Spirit

We made sure that our children were present when the Holy Spirit was moving in a unique or powerful way. Sometimes that meant they would be up later at night than was our custom. It didn't matter. Being exposed to a move of God, with the possibility of a divine encounter, is a million times more important to me than how well they would do the next day. If I kept them up too late, we'd require much less from them in the morning. It's important that they learn from us what's really important. And sometimes they learn what's important by watching what is inconvenient for us, yet we remain faithful in pursuing. My children's lives were shaped by these experiences. We owe it to them to make sure they are in the room when God is doing something extraordinary.

Word of God

We read God's Word as a family. But probably equally important was they were able to witness Beni and me reading the Word on our own. They follow examples more than they follow commands.

Worship

This is our reason for being—we are worshipers. We would reward our children for participating in worship in the corporate gathering. Ice cream works wonders. Some would complain at this, but it didn't matter to us. Our children were involved, which had an effect on their character and behavior. To correct for bad behavior but not reward for the good is a perverted system. They also learned something that many adults have forgotten. *"He who comes to God must believe that He is and that He is a rewarder of those who seek Him"* (Heb. 11:6). He rewards. So I must do the same to represent Him well.

Fellowship

We spent quality time with others. Oftentimes these were families with children the ages of ours. But sometimes it wasn't. It could be a grandma and grandpa or even some singles. The point was, they needed to see what it's like to value people and interact with them. Fellowship really is an exchange of life. Spending time with people, showing them value, learning to receive from them, and learning to give to them help to shape the heart brilliantly.

Rest

I live a fairly intense lifestyle. With the travel and local responsibilities, things can get pretty extreme. Rest is one of the true joys of life. I loved spending time with my children and my wife, unwinding. Sometimes we'll go away for a few days. Sometimes we'll just sit and watch our favorite TV show. But the point is, rest is essential. In a performance culture, people want to apologize when they need rest. Don't. It's a provision of the Lord. It's also essential for me as it is in rest that I often become more aware of the presence of God, communing with Him in ways that are more challenging in the busyness of life.

Play

We did things together often. Parks, playgrounds, and other recreational activities were a part of our life. As they got older, they participated in sports. It was such a joy to watch them play. We also developed hobbies together, which is a beautiful way to connect. Hunting and fishing were a part of our routine. But so was throwing the baseball or football on the front lawn. It is life. It is to be healthy and fun, all as an offering to the Lord.

WHAT WE KNOW

We instinctively know that when we give money to help the poor, or to support our local church or another project for the Kingdom, the gift has a supernatural effect. That really is an amazing truth. The money we all hold in our hands has been used for so many things. Some of them good, like groceries, clothing, and food. But it has also been used for drugs, pornography, etc. And that money is now in my hands, and through generosity I can shape the course of history with it, as it will surely bring forth fruit for His glory. The profound conclusion is that the natural becomes supernaturally effective through giving. But what would happen if we did the same with our family time, our work schedule, our fellowship, etc.? It's the same concept. That which we gave to Him becomes supernaturally effective because it was placed into His hands as a gift. Our efforts that may seem so insignificant are very similar to the boy's lunch. It was enough to feed a child. But once it was placed in the Master's hands, it became supernaturally effective enough to feed a multitude. So is every offering we give to Him as we learn to worship in all areas of life.

Chapter Fourteen

GENEROSITY OF HEART

As mentioned earlier, I grew up with a high value for generosity. My parents and grandparents were extremely generous. Sometimes we don't realize how much we are influenced by our own family values until you see how other people live in response to their own challenges. That is the case with this subject. My parents constantly served others with their money, time, and acts of kindness. They were generous with their words as well.

Our home was never a place where I heard them speak unfavorably of another. I don't ever remember sitting at the dinner table and hearing my parents speak critically of another person, whether it was a board member who was causing division or another pastor in town who was publically criticizing my father. He was generous in conversation because he was generous in heart. It's how kings live. I do think it's time to recognize our royal assignment and avoid the pettiness in much conversation that is beneath our royal call.

HEARING FROM GOD

Heaven's culture is not formed in us beyond our heart to hear His voice. That is where life begins for us. We live *"by every word that proceeds from His mouth"* (see Matt. 4:4).

The Lord used two areas to teach me how to recognize His voice. The first was reading the Scriptures. The Bible is God's Word. It is absolute in authority and carries the revelation we need for all of life. I tell our students, "The Bible is Jesus in print. Don't tell me you love Jesus, but you don't love His Word."

I noticed in my early years that God would speak to me as I'd read the Bible. Verses or subjects and sometimes simple phrases seemed to leap off the page and touch my heart so deeply. The words literally came alive! It fed my soul in ways that are nearly impossible to describe. Oftentimes, I would not have been able to explain what I had just read, as it hadn't touched my mind yet. My heart was always moved to greater surrender, a deeper sense of awe for who He is, and greater hunger for Him and His Word. My mind would eventually catch up.

I knew enough to be able to say that His Word gave me life. It became more and more obvious that there was a treasure found on those pages that was far greater than I had ever experienced before. I remember as a young man picking a book off the shelf of our church library. I was not much of a reader at the time, but the appearance of the book stood out to me. I can still see it. It was very old, maybe 6 by 4 inches in size, a white hardback with gold print on the cover. I randomly opened to a page and started reading out of curiosity and actually felt life pour into me. I thought immediately, *Who wrote this book? This is amazing!* As I looked for the author, I discovered that I was actually reading a portion of Scripture that the author put in his book to prove his point. It was a strong lesson for me. His Word gives life. And I felt it when it happened. While that may not happen all the time, recognize and celebrate when it does.

I often hear people say, "I don't remember what I read." My response is always the same: "I don't remember what I had for breakfast two weeks ago either, but it still nourished me. Just read with a surrendered heart, and you'll be amazed at what He does in you over time."

As I would give time to pray and study the passage He highlighted for me, God would open it up and give me understanding. It seemed to always reveal His ways, His heart, and His purpose in the earth. The result was always that my heart would burn for His Word even more, as it does to this day.

When God would speak to me, it was through the Word, not in addition to His Word. This needs to be said. Some might think that adding to the Bible is okay. It's not okay. Ever. And then there are some who accuse us of adding to God's Word, simply because we believe God still speaks. Neither is true or healthy.

The second area that God used to teach me how to recognize His voice was in giving. This was so fascinating to me, as He always seemed to make it clear what I was to give for a specific cause or situation. With His voice comes the faith to obey. Learning to give according to His heart is always beyond what my mind would lead me to. So faith was essential. This is where I learned that *"faith comes by hearing"* (Rom. 10:17 NKJV). Learning His voice in the area of money has been monumental for me, as the effect of that lesson has spilled over into other areas of my life. Knowing His voice is one of the great treasures of life. Simply put, He speaks, and we live.

I remember the Lord speaking to me about supporting a specific missionary. The amount was clear. But I also knew we didn't have that much money to give on a monthly basis, which was the direction of the Lord. I obeyed. Within a few days, my car insurance company sent me a letter apologizing for overcharging me for my monthly rate. They lowered it, almost to the exact amount of my pledge. Coincidence? Perhaps. But they seem to happen more often when I obey.

Stories of this nature are simple but common in my life. Learning to impart this as a cultural value is necessary but can never be reduced to a one-time act. The lifestyle of generosity must be taught and modeled. The reason is not because of the Church's need for money. While that is a constant, the real impact comes from the way we live for others. Money is one of the tools used to reveal the Father's heart and can impact the value system of entire cities.

BIRTHDAYS ARE FUN!

Many years ago, I decided to give gifts to my family members on my birthday. We have a big party, and I hand out gifts to my three children, their wonderful spouses, and my ten grandchildren. It's a highlight of the whole year for me. It is the moment when I feel the most like Santa. It is such a fun time. And I've noticed that my whole family loves my birthday. Ha!

During the year, I pay attention to their interests so that when the time comes for my birthday party, I can sow into their God-given abilities and interests. I only have one life to live. Which means I only have one lifetime to reveal what our heavenly Father is like. *"God so loved the world, that He gave"* (John 3:16).

CORPORATE GENEROSITY

When I first became pastor of Bethel Church in Redding, California, I noticed that the finances of the church were in bad shape. I knew enough to know that problems in this area are often symptomatic of problems elsewhere. It was obvious to me that I would need to teach on the subject. So I did. The first two weeks in my new assignment at Bethel, the teaching was about money.

I have purposed never to teach on a subject for personal gain. And while there are times it seems to be unavoidable, I try to put parameters in place to guarantee that the teaching is always for the benefit of others.

I taught for two weeks on the tithe. I know it's become popular in recent days to state that the tithe was from the law, and we are free from the law. Therefore, this must mean we are free from the tithe. While tithing isn't the subject of this book, I will take a moment to put this story into a context:

First of all, the tithe was not from the Law. It was Abraham who first instituted the practice of the tithe. In Scripture, he is called the father of our faith. (See Romans 4.) Many years later it was ratified by the Law and was later ratified by Jesus Himself. History shows us it was also the practice of the early Church fathers, which speaks to us of the culture Jesus gave them. So it is with joy and confidence I teach on the tithe and offerings as important expressions of how I acknowledge and honor the Lordship of Jesus in my life. The fruit in my own life in this area is beyond debate. We also have practiced this as a ministry where we tithe to other ministries from which we receive no direct benefit.

At the end of the second week of teaching, I called for a repentance offering. To prove our repentance is real, it must bear fruit. Otherwise, it can be just a momentary attitude of the heart. I then informed the people that we would not be keeping the money from this offering. We'd be giving the entire amount to another church in our area. The repentance was deep, as the offering was unusually large.

I called another pastor in the city and asked if we could have lunch together. After sitting down to eat, I handed him a large check and told him the story. He looked at the amount, and then told me he wasn't sure if it was exact, but it was close to the amount that they were behind in their bills at church. This was so encouraging to me. But it's what happened next that touched me even more deeply.

He went to his church board with our gift. They were so moved that they decided to do the same, but give their entire Easter Sunday offerings to other churches in town. That offering was three times larger than their average! They divided it among three other ministries. One of those ministries had a bus ministry that brought the kids from around the city to their very special children's ministry. They were so moved by this act of kindness toward them that they followed suit by giving their best bus to another church in town that also had a bus ministry. I hope you get the point. Generosity is contagious. It is Kingdom. And it reveals the Father. And while a single act of generosity does not create culture, it does set a direction in thought, attitude, and practice that eventually becomes our culture.

DISCIPLE NATIONS

We have to make sure that we require ourselves to think bigger than we find to be comfortable. God has not called us to do what is humanly possible or reasonable. We are children of a King who knows no impossibility. And He longs for His heart to become ours.

As I stated earlier, the American church spends something like 95 percent of its income on itself. Practically put, our focus is on caring for ourselves. We build buildings, create programs, hire staff, and the like to take care of ourselves. While those percentages concern me, I really love the privilege of caring for ourselves. It truly is a joy, as you can measure the impact of your giving rather quickly when the people you love and spend time with receive the greatest impact of your giving. But at the same time, this behavior reveals how little the average believer is aware of our international responsibility. Jim Elliott, who himself was martyred for the Gospel, said, "The light that shines the farthest, shines the brightest at home." That is one of my all-time favorite quotes. It basically says that those who reach out to the nations through giving, love, and care will always have enough to meet the needs of those in their own circle of influence. I do believe that and have practiced that for well over 45 years.

GIVING IN PRAYER

One of the things I began to do 40 years ago for the church we pastored in the mountain community of Weaverville, California, was to teach them to pray for nations. I knew if they obtained God's heart for nations, the giving would follow. It was an interesting journey together. We started late-night prayer meetings every Friday night. We always spent an hour or so in worship and then prayed for our city. And sometime during that second hour we'd pick a nation to pray for. We'd then give ourselves to an extended period of time of intercession for that nation, always praying for the church planted in that nation as well as for their political leaders. Our people were so good in following this direction. Even if they didn't have the vision for these nations, they'd do their best to pray.

Not only would we cast vision for nations in prayer, I'd also bring in missionary friends to speak at the church to share their heart for another nation. It became contagious. Soon the spirit of prayer would come upon us as we'd pray for our city and then for a nation. Following the Holy Spirit in prayer is a great way to learn of His heart for nations. Jesus taught us so much during this time. But it was about five years after starting this direction that I had one of our members come to me and say, "I get it. I finally get it." Her response was actually an indication of a corporate breakthrough. Not everything is fully grasped simply because it was taught and practiced. It often takes day after day, week after week of living a God-given mandate before it actually becomes a part of who we are. That is the point at which we can call something *culture*. Values practiced over time become culture. Our small group of believers started to think about nations. And perhaps more importantly, they began to think that one person and God were a majority.

You have to understand—people came to our community of 3,500 people to retire, withdraw, or escape. While that wasn't true of everyone, it does represent a vast majority. The thought of living for a group of people they'd probably never see in this lifetime was a new and scary concept. But it is totally Kingdom in its nature. And when embraced, it helps define the nature of the culture you live in and impart.

In my final year of pastoring Mountain Chapel, we actually had somewhere around 100 people go somewhere in the world to serve with the Gospel. Some of them were gone for a week. Others served for a year or more. The point is that valuing nations changed how we lived.

YOU'RE HEALTHY—NOW WHAT?

We want all believers and their households to be healthy and productive. That's likely why we spend the 95 percent on ourselves. We have a vision for it. It's a very real need to have entire communities model healthy relationships, productivity, prosperity with purpose, providing a place where children can freely grow up with dreams, with adults who contribute to their destinies. Our philosophy basically comes down to this: Once you're healthy and happy, we want you deployed into your world-changing role. It doesn't matter to us if you're a missionary to a foreign field, a dentist or a doctor, a stay-at-home mom, or a pastor—fill in the blanks. Do what's in your heart, and do it as unto the Lord. But from that position, think of the significance of your role as God breathes on your labor and station in life. What could happen? Dream and obey to find out what might be possible in your lifetime.

Once again, work is worship. This is a significant part of the reformation in thought and practice that we are seeing unfold before us. I truly believe that this is part of what will help us bring about the greatest revival the world has ever seen.

THE CULTURE OF GENEROSITY

Generosity has become a part of our influence in the city, and in many ways around the world. As soon as someone on our staff gets breakthrough in an area, we invest them in the nations. They are given time each quarter, and sometimes each month, to travel. They are not punished financially for this opportunity. We have learned that you can only keep what you give away. And we want to give away our best for the benefit of others. This, of course, is always done with keeping the health of the local church in mind. We're just not stingy with our own people.

Our commitment to waiters and waitresses in our city has reached a very high level. In the USA, the wages of the restaurant help are small. It's the tips that really help them make ends meet. We have taught and practiced generosity in this area for as long as I can remember.

My own children practiced this even in their teenage years. I heard of times when they were going out to eat with their friends following an evening service. They would see how much money they had and then would only order what would leave them with enough money to leave a radically generous tip. They sacrificed to protect their heart of generosity.

Our own people who work in the restaurant business have told us that we are the topic of conversation after we leave the restaurant. It's the way we honor the staff of servers that has left a mark on their lives. Even owners have thanked us for the way we have impacted their business. I once brought several dozen people to one of our nicer restaurants. At the end of the evening I thanked an owner for the excellent service his staff provided for us. His response surprised me a bit. "You trained them. They're your people." They were people who had been trained in the values of the Kingdom, and they took it seriously enough to practice it at work. Even owners value the beauty of the Kingdom of God.

This lifestyle must affect everything about our lives—from actions to thoughts and plans and ambitions. Everything we are and have must come under the Lordship of Jesus to accurately display who our Father is and what His Kingdom is like.

Chapter Fifteen

KINGDOM OF ABUNDANCE

Heaven has the ultimate culture of abundance. It is not only a place of "more than enough"; it is a place of extravagance and extremes. Learning about His world and how this knowledge is to affect our attitudes and expectations is an important part of the *"on earth as it is in heaven"* mandate. I know that there are some who at this point hear me say "materialism." And I understand this reaction as there has been much error as it pertains to money. Yet the reality of Heaven is still to permeate this world, regardless of the errors of others. *No use* is no better than *misuse*. For what it's worth, materialism is a poor representation of God's world because it fails to represent His heart.

PRACTICAL AND NORMAL

Many believers don't actually know how to live life in a practical way. They understand church attendance, serving in a ministry, and other essentials of that nature, but they really don't know how practical God is. They choose to give attention to what seems to be spiritual, never learning that the natural often reveals the nature of the unseen world. When God gave Israel rules to live by, He was often showing them how His creation works. And to get His creation to serve you well, enabling you to prosper, they needed to pay attention to the rules of the designer.

It still astounds me that God's idea of paradise, the Promised Land, was a place where His people would have to work. Work is a pleasure in His eyes, and it is an expression of worship. Once again, we discover the subject of co-laboring with God. As we work, He breathes on our labor and the natural becomes supernaturally productive in ways that bless us and glorify Him.

This, of course, was under God's favor, but it was still work. In doing so, they would create wealth. God's idea of living on blessed land was to work hard and make blessed wages. God made His people to be the head and not the tail, the lender and not the borrower, and gave them the power to make wealth. Those realities are as true today as they've ever been. But people often misapply or misunderstand Jesus' teaching on money. Tragically, this misapplication of truth has cost generations their place of influence.

THE PRACTICAL WILL OF GOD

When the apostle Paul taught Timothy about God's will for people's daily lives, he got really practical. He started with a prayer direction, but then transitioned into revealing the wonderful outcome of the prayer direction. This is found in First Timothy 2:1-4:

> *First of all, then, I urge that entreaties and prayers, petitions and thanksgivings, be made on behalf of all men, for kings and all who are in authority, so **that we may lead a tranquil and quiet life** in all godliness and dignity. This is good and acceptable in the sight of God our Savior,*

who desires all men to be saved and to come to the knowledge of the truth.

The direction for our lives is simple but important. Pray for all in authority, with thankfulness. It is usually fairly easy to pray for those in authority, but it's not always easy to be thankful for them. When we consider that Paul lived at a time of extremely abusive leaders, we realize that this was not an untested theory or a flowery suggestion. His insight has teeth to it because of his own experience. Cultivating a heart that values leaders regardless of how little godliness is in their lives is a challenge, but with great reward. Being thankful for them before they deserve it qualifies them for a visitation of God in a most remarkable way.

I happen to know of cases where this was done, and the most vile and wicked leaders changed into servants of the people. I also know of times when millions of dollars in bribe money was returned or donated to their communities, just because people loved them and honored these leaders into their rightful place of righteous influence. It is not my place to mention these leaders or countries. But I can promote Ed Silvoso and his incredible ministry of bringing trans-formation to cities and nations. His materials inspire all who read them as they are filled with insight and testimonies where his bib-lical teaching has extraordinary fruit, like the examples given above. And he correctly stewards many of these stories to the glory of God. Search them out.

Look again at the scriptures quoted above. God's will is a *tranquil and quiet life*. Tranquil means *free from disturbance*. And quiet means *uninterrupted*. That is the heart of God for every city on earth—that His purpose for our wellbeing would be without disturbance and interruption. That alone should appeal to everyone reading this book. In that atmosphere, there is a future and a hope. What a profound outcome for those praying for their leaders.

If we can celebrate simplicity, God can trust us with the complex because we won't be impressed or controlled by it. Seeing the supernatural interventions of God only in the extraordinary can create an addiction to the spectacular and not to God Himself. For this reason, we call this a relational journey, as He constantly monitors our heart for Him and not just what He does. The ordinary, when cared for *as unto the Lord,* is the school for the extraordinary. Thankful stewards are always ready for increase into the more obvious supernatural displays of God's grace.

That kind of life is not something we're supposed to wait for to enjoy in Heaven. The way we pray for leaders influences the outcome here and now. And if a tranquil and quiet life in all godliness and dignity wasn't enough, it is done with the salvation of souls as the ultimate target. Consider this: The will of God, revealed in a peace-filled lifestyle, is to be what attracts *"**all men to be saved** and come to the knowledge of the truth."* *All men to be saved* is our primary target. But even the greatest of all miracles, the salvation of a soul, is to set the stage for *coming to the knowledge of the truth.* This enables us as a healthy society to build upon this lifestyle of peace for future generations. Solomon had a chance at this but missed it due to his sin. This knowledge enables us to help design a godly culture and create a momentum for the future generations to enjoy.

DESIGNED FOR BEAUTY AND PLEASURE

At the center of God's own heart is a love for beauty and pleasure. He created all things for Himself to enjoy and for His creation to delight in Him. There is no delight, beauty, or pleasure outside of Him that can satisfy the cry of our hearts.

He designed the sunrise and the sunset. The stars shine at His command, revealing His delight in the sons and daughters of God. He created the baby's smile and the elderly's laughter. He is the God of beauty and design and has called us into the co-laboring role to put our mark on what He has made. Just as Adam gave names to all the animals, so God has invited us into a relational role of creativity, enhancing the beauty of His creation. This truly represents the joy of the journey and an abundance of heart.

PROSPERITY OF SOUL

This subject is addressed openly in Third John, but spoken of by implication throughout the Bible, especially the Psalms.

> *Beloved, I pray that in all respects you may prosper and be*
> *in good health, just as your soul prospers* (3 John 2).

I never tire of this verse, as the implications are so rich and fulfilling. I love to see how one part of our lives has an effect on another. Our inner world, in this case a soul that overflows in abundance, has an effect on our outer world in areas of health and finances. There is wisdom to be learned in paying attention to these principles. This really is remarkable as God wants me to be healthy on the inside, knowing it will take care of many of the things I look for on the outside.

Our soul is most commonly defined as our will, our mind, and our emotions. Those three areas are to experience and discover what prosperity looks like from God's perspective.

Will

Practically speaking, what does it look like to be healthy and prosperous in our will? Many people want to do the right thing, but they carry a pressure connected to the opinions of others. It's not that a calloused heart is the answer, as we're to value the good counsel. But there is a fear of man that poisons many people's ability to be bold and obey God. They find it difficult to choose the right thing because of this pressure. Jesus addressed this issue as it pertains to our faith. *"How can you believe, when you receive glory from one another and you do not seek the glory that is from the one and only God?"* (John 5:44). Our faith is compromised anytime we look for the approval of man over the approval of God. Healthy souls have no attachments that would keep their will from the will of God. They have no indebtedness to others in an unhealthy way. Conversely, the healthy soul knows the value of godly counsel and knows how to benefit from the courage of others. Sometimes it's in the context of partnering with trusted friends that we find our greatest breakthroughs. Choosing to fellowship with people who make us stronger is wise, as it provides us with a momentum for great faith and the ability to stand alone when the moment calls for it.

Mind

So what does it look like to be prosperous in our mind? It's been said countless times that the battleground is in our minds. This is so true. Just recognizing that gives us an advantage, as we then become conscious of the fact that the enemy of our souls loves to contradict God's Word to cause us to stray from God's will. Not only is a prosperous mind more immune to lies, it thinks creatively. To use an accounting analogy, we are out of the red (debt) and into the black (profit). Whenever we are burdened with worry or anxiety, we are less likely to think with fresh creative solutions and less likely to join in the divine adventure offered to us. Part of the devil's primary focus is to get us anxious over the issues of life. If I get anxious, he has successfully shut down my ability to represent our Father, the creator of all, through inspired thought. The command *"do not fear"* is the most frequently given command in the Bible. It's repeated the most often because fear is the number-one tool the enemy uses to dislocate us from our purpose in life. Fear plagues the mind with unnecessary weight to carry, removing us from the creative expression we were designed for.

On the other hand, perfect love drives out fear. This must be more than a biblical truth, as important as that is. It must become our experience to truly drive out fear. And you'll know when that has happened as your trust in Him becomes the overriding expression of your thought life.

Emotions

What does an emotionally healthy life look like? First of all, this starts with a view of our past. All of my yesterdays are under the blood of Jesus. That means I am forgiven, and I stand before the Father as one who is perfectly clean. We must see our past the way the Father does—through His redemptive work of Jesus. Revisiting our past apart from the blood of Jesus is to subject ourselves to an emotional experience separate from reality. It is deception. Think about this. If I have turned to Jesus in repentance, I am forgiven. Any view of my past that doesn't include forgiveness is inaccurate. The grace of God must come into view anytime I look backwards. Otherwise, I subject myself to deception, as I am visiting something in my memories that no longer exists. Knowing we are forgiven, and forgiving ourselves, is key to healthy emotions. The devil works to keep us in guilt, shame, and regret. This is the enemy's focus as these are areas I have no legal access to, as Jesus bought it with His own life. Putting my attention on the past without the blood of Jesus ensures I will be in continual frustration. It's like having an itch that you can't scratch. You have no ability to fix the past that is already fixed. Healthy emotions live from the state of wholeness.

When we are truly healthy in our hearts, anyone from our past can walk into the room, and it doesn't cause us to falter in our faith.

It is also true that people who are healthy emotionally tend to live from what God has said about them. Meditating on God's Word doesn't just help the mind. It helps us in our hearts. It strengthens us emotionally into a healthy place of abundance.

FEAR OF MAN

Let me make a few more comments about the fear of man, as this is a primary source of poverty of soul. First of all, it's important to realize that the devil can't create. He can only distort. If he can't get me to fall through weakness, he tries to get me to fall through misuse of my strengths. Peter was known for his boldness. When this gift was misused, he spoke out of turn, rebuked Jesus concerning His upcoming crucifixion, and boldly confessed he didn't know Jesus while He was headed to the cross. His gift was his point of personal failure. But when that gift operates under the Lordship of Jesus, we see him standing before a crowd of several thousand, many of whom were mockers, preaching the Gospel with boldness. This resulted in the conversion of several thousand people. Those who struggle most often with the fear of man are usually people who have a gift of discerning the hearts of others. This person becomes unusually aware of the ideas, opinions, and convictions of others. Using this gift correctly, this person is able to serve well, and they know the tender areas of another person's heart. But this gift outside of the Lordship of Jesus causes them to react to what they discern and fall under the influence of an unredeemed mind. When the discerning heart is used correctly, they are no longer intimidated by the opinions of others, but are instead positioned to serve that one who tends to control others by their stance on issues. The issue at hand is the Lordship of Jesus. And that really is the key to a healthy soul.

EXTREME PROSPERITY OF SOUL

When God talks about prosperity of soul, there is no ceiling or limit to what He has made available to us all. His Kingdom is eternal and without limits. Therefore, His desire for our inner world is greater than our picture of the wealthiest person in the world. Bill Gates, for example, retired from work at Microsoft only to figure out how to give his wealth away. He has summoned some of the wealthiest people in the world to this honorable lifestyle as philanthropists. Is it possible to have prosperity of soul that is equal to what these people have in money? I think so. I can't imagine anyone's wealth, including Solomon's, surpassing what God intended for every believer in their inner world.

Let's look at the philanthropist's dilemma more closely. They are challenged with the task of giving away money responsibly. They know firsthand the tragedies that happen when too much is given to the wrong person or organization. Money becomes the fuel for self-destruction. But done correctly, that same amount of money becomes the building block to a better future, often for entire cities or even countries. Now consider what that mindset looks like when it refers to an extreme abundance of our inner world. Could this be what Paul is drawing upon?

> *When you assemble, each one has a psalm, has a teaching, has a revelation, has a tongue, has an interpretation. Let all things be done for edification* (1 Corinthians 14:26).

And also:

> *Let the word of Christ richly dwell within you, with all wisdom teaching and admonishing one another with psalms and hymns and spiritual songs, singing with thankfulness in your hearts to God* (Colossians 3:16).

Do you see it? When we assemble together, we are to come ready to give things away for the encouragement and strengthening of others. This is a picture of a person with a healthy inner world. They have such abundance of heart that they have to prepare ahead of time how they're going to give away what they've been given. It may mean an encouraging word or a promise from Scripture. It might also mean laying hands on someone for healing or releasing the peace of God that you carry. The application of this truth is limitless. It also doesn't mean that the prosperous soul no longer receives, as that limits our strength and courage. When we learn to continually receive, we reinforce our strength and awareness that we are a body. But it does mean we stop coming just to receive.

God wants us to be mature. A baby's life is all about them. They cry, and people show up to help them. They are the focus of the household, and rightly so. But if a 20-year-old acts that way, it's no longer cute. Maturity is in part measured by our ability to contribute to our surroundings. And our maturity is so profoundly connected to a prosperous inner world that it can be measured by what we give and the strength we provide for others.

TAKE ANOTHER LOOK

Let's take one more look at this verse:

> *Beloved, I pray that in all respects you may prosper and be in good health, just as your soul prospers* (3 John 2).

This scripture profoundly connects our outward measure of blessing to what's happening on the inside of us. Let me be more specific. What is happening inside of us has a direct effect on our financial life as well as our health. This is Bible.

This reality has been tapped into even by non-believers. I know of people who have had terminal diseases, who have chosen to watch a continual stream of funny movies. They literally laughed and laughed for weeks at a time, only to discover their disease disappeared.

I heard Randy Clark once say, "Laughter is to salvation what weeping is to repentance." That is such a powerful statement, as it gives a logical place for both expressions. Yet the Church often rejects the expression of corporate joy, calling it disorderly and unbiblical. The Bible says, *"In [His] presence is fullness of joy"* (Ps. 16:11). Isn't it possible for laughter to be included in the biblical description of the *fullness of joy?* Is it not at least a part of this vast subject? I think so. And we suffer in our inner world because we end up cutting off

God's prescription of joy from our experience in God. "Laughter is good medicine" and *the kingdom of God is...righteousness and peace and joy*" (Rom. 14:17).

Two thirds of Kingdom expression is felt—*peace and joy*. Enjoying God and His Kingdom is the key to a healthy inner world. His Kingdom provides us with a cultural mandate and expression.

PROSPERITY HAS A PURPOSE

I find it interesting that a biblical subject like prosperity can bring such strong reactions. Reaction to error usually creates another error. This time the error is more socially acceptable to our peers and friends. Yet it is no less an error. Responding to a biblical subject with a willingness to learn is essential to correctly approaching the subjects we have seen abused or taught incorrectly. Reacting almost never accomplishes what we hope, although it makes us feel zealous and worthy.

Stewarding blessing and increase well should be the intention of every believer. If abundance is a normal Kingdom expression, we should prepare for increase with prayers and study on the subjects we anticipate God's blessing in.

The two most obvious subjects implied in the 3 John 2 passage are money and health, although I believe there is reason to apply this principle to relationships, legacy, church life, community health, and more. I'll stick with the two most obvious for now. Money in the Kingdom requires that I consider how to have an eternal impact through my giving, wise spending, and investing. Each action can bring definition and purpose to the abundance God has given us. When it comes to health, it requires me to take proper care of the body I've been given. For Beni and me, it means we eat healthy organic foods, we work out and exercise, we take appropriate supplements to help provide nutrients that may be missing from our diet, and we protect our rest. These areas are essential to obtaining and maintaining a healthy lifestyle. It's interesting that there are many people who would never steal or commit adultery, yet have no problem ignoring our need for Sabbath rest. It's in the same list of commandments. Health in our spirit, soul, and body is profoundly connected to our obedience to His commands.

PERSONAL NOTE

I celebrate hiddenness. Do not seek to be known. Being known by many or even celebrated by many is not necessarily a good thing. When we stand before God, we will treasure most the moments when we honored God and no one saw it. Those are moments when He honors us most. Treasure hiddenness for as long as He allows you to remain there. When the Lord unveils you, celebrate that too, as it is a work of God. His promotions are beautiful and carry no ill effects. But if we look to be unknown to avoid responsibility, it works against the purpose of God in our lives. Embrace the season you're in.

If I see an article in a magazine or newspaper where I played a significant role in an event and my name is mentioned, I give thanks for the honor. I've learned that with the increase of favor comes the increase of opposition. According Bob Weiner, "The more income, the more tax." That has been my experience. But, if my name is not mentioned, I celebrate being hidden more than when my name is mentioned. Choose carefully what you allow to move your heart.

BLESSING ATTRACTS

A simple reminder at this point might be helpful. The prayer of Psalm 67 is clear: *"Bless* [me]...*that Your way may be known on the earth, Your salvation among all nations"* (Ps. 67:1-2). Living a highly favored life attracts people to the God we serve. We are supposed to model life under the reign and rule of a perfect Father. This is the culture of Heaven made practical for all those who look at our lives. For some, the only Bible they will ever read will be the well-lived life of a child of God. Let's make sure that what they read in us represents Him well.

Chapter Sixteen

PERSONAL FULFILLMENT AND THE CROSS

Revealing the heart of the Father is the key for building a culture with a value system that reflects the culture of Heaven. It's impossible to succeed at this endeavor if we ignore what God doesn't ignore. And in this case, we need to pay attention to the fulfillment of our personal purpose and design. This becomes clearly manifested through the hearts of the surrendered believers.

One of the areas for which we have a high value is joy, fun, and pleasure. I know it doesn't sound Christian to many, but I believe it is when done correctly. Those are things He designed us for, and in doing so He is glorified by us when we live according to design.

I discovered a long time ago if I'm not having fun, I need to reevaluate what I'm doing. That's not to say that everything we experience in life is fun. It isn't. But there's always joy to be found in the journey, as joy is an expression of the Kingdom of God (see Rom. 14:17). And the Kingdom is always at hand—joy is always within reach.

Our relationship with God must bear the fruit of His nature, which is a perfect and complete delight in us as His creation. It is recorded that Jesus had more joy than everyone around Him put together. (See Hebrews 1:9 and John 15:11.) And that joy was expressed by Him on the way to the cross. If anyone has ever had an excuse for not having joy, it would have to be Jesus about to be crucified. He set the standard, and He is the only one worth following.

THE VALUE OF HUMOR

One of the things that becomes increasingly evident the more time you spend in our world is that we give great value to humor. We laugh a lot—at jokes, at our mistakes, at just about everything. Laughter gives a great reprieve from the everyday affairs of life.

In my early years, I was intense and serious in my quest to follow Jesus. I think my picture of Jesus was more similar to Spock on *Star Trek* than what is in Scripture. After all, what could be more serious that holiness, hell, making it to heaven, etc.? When we were first married, Beni used to tell me to go for a walk and pray. She knew I'd be less intense after spending time with Jesus. I thought that's what real disciples did with their lives—get intense, focused, and serious about everything in life. But it didn't work. I was miserable, and I was determined to make everyone around me miserable, too. It seemed to me that this is what holiness looked like. I thought this was how I could prove to be a disciple of Jesus. It sounds so funny now, but it was truer than I really care to admit. It finally became clear to me that time spent in the presence of God did not make me more intense in a self-critical way. I came out of those times refreshed and happy. And because *"the joy of the Lord is your strength"* (Neh. 8:10), it can be said that *we are no stronger than our joy.*

The heart of God for our personal fulfillment in life is bigger than we can imagine. That's why He has covenanted with us to go *"beyond all we could ask or think"* (see Eph. 3:20). He is that kind of

Father. But the Kingdom of God works differently from anything we're accustomed to. As a result, it is easy for the natural mind to come to the opposite conclusion about God.

In His Kingdom, we do the following: die to self, live humbly, give sacrificially, exhibit boldness when it will create opposition, suffer for doing the right thing, resist defending ourselves, accept being misunderstood, etc. The list of specific acts and attitudes that appear to be anything but personal fulfillment is long. Very long. But the heart of the Father remains set on our fulfillment. But once again, it is only accomplished His way. If He honors our desires apart from our surrender to His ways, He builds in us a greater bent toward carnality. And that is the poorest of foundations upon which to build His eternal purposes. He's a much better builder than that.

TREE OF LIFE

Earlier in this book I addressed the fascinating offers that Jesus gave to His disciples that had previously only been given to Solomon. Four times in three chapters Jesus basically invited them to ask for anything they wanted and it would be done for them. Solomon was given this offer once. The followers of Jesus are given this *blank check* as a daily gift to reveal the glory of His design of partnering with His creation.

We know that this blank check isn't about God inviting us to new levels of selfishness under the guise of the name of Jesus. But neither is He making us into machines who only pray what He commands us to pray. If that were true the invitation would have been a command, and might have sounded more like, *"Only ask for what I tell you to ask for!"* What stands out to me the most is the vulnerability of God Himself, who is the perfect Father. He invites us into the courts of Heaven to dialogue with Him about what is to happen on planet Earth, the place He has given to us to steward (see Ps. 115:16). This is not a little matter. Somewhere in that equation is the free will of man merging with the dreams and desires of God. In some ways, this is the essence of beauty—the brilliance of the creator seen in the co-laboring functionality of those made in His image. It is by this fulfillment of purpose and design that God is glorified.

> If you abide in Me, and My words abide in you, **ask whatever you wish, and it will be done for you. My Father is glorified by this**, that you bear much fruit, and so prove to be My disciples (John 15:7-8).

The fruit mentioned in this passage is answer to prayer. And it is the fulfillment of those desires that brings God the greatest glory and becomes the evidence of our relationship with God—*and so prove to be My disciples.*

Once again, the book of divine wisdom brings out the beauty of God's plan. *"Hope deferred makes the heart sick, but desire fulfilled is a tree of life"* (Prov. 13:12). Disappointment makes us vulnerable to spiritual diseases like discouragement, depression, introspection, and resentment. Thankfully it's not automatic. The outcome of disappointment is determined by how well we manage our hearts (see Prov. 4:23). And while the first half of this verse is the part most often quoted, it's the second half that reveals God's intention and design for us. It's not a stretch to call this phrase, "God's will for our lives." It is in this passage we gain understanding of a mysterious part of the Garden of Eden called the Tree of Life.

It's important to remember when Adam and Eve sinned, an angel protected them from partaking from the Tree of Life. It's quite possible that eating from this tree would have made their sinful condition eternal. If that is true, it could be said that the Tree of Life marks people for eternity—as in *eternal purpose.* When merging the themes found in Genesis and Proverbs, it becomes apparent that part of God's plan for us is the enjoyment of fulfilled dreams and desires. In this passage, that idea is recognized as a part of our *eternal purpose.* I know at first glance this appears to be contrary to the teaching on the need to bear our cross daily, which is one of the most necessary teachings for our life in Christ. And while it may *seem* contrary to the *cross walk*, it is not contrary to the *resurrection life* that the cross leads us to. This reveals original design.

Fulfillment in life is always through surrender to His purposes and is found through our fellowship with Him. We were created to enjoy personal fulfillment as a part of God's original design. The Holy Spirit through Solomon reveals one of the primary features of the Tree of Life. It was to bring life, strength, and eternal purpose.

PLEASURE BY DESIGN

The quest for personal fulfillment often takes people in every direction but the right one. The stories of tragic pursuits surround us daily. And yet the Father, who is perfect in every possible way, has designed us for a life of personal fulfillment. But it only works His way. His rules are not confining in the sense of punishment or unhealthy restrictions. They are empowering, as they connect us with His original design. You could probably build a table by using a crescent wrench as hammer, but it's not according to design, and would no doubt take longer with many mistakes. The point is, our basic trust must be in the one who designed us for pleasure—His and ours.

The picture that comes to mind of this reality is when a person frantically tries to catch a butterfly. They are so erratic in flight that they are difficult to catch. But if you remain still, it just might land on you. Personal fulfillment happens by pursuing the right things in God's value system. A better way to put it is personal fulfillment is not found in the pursuit of personal fulfillment. It is the product or fruit of pursuing God's heart and purposes for our lives. It becomes the butterfly that lands on the person of rest, who is not frantically driven by their own needs or agendas but instead becomes increasingly hungry for God and His Kingdom—His divine order. This really is another way of practicing *"seek first the kingdom of God...and all these things shall be added to you"* (Matt. 6:33 NKJV).

THE FIELD OF DREAMS, THE BOOK OF DREAMS

I wish I had started the discipline of writing down my dreams in my youth. I didn't realize He was the kind of Father who wanted to know what was in my heart. You might point out to me that He already knows my dreams and doesn't need my list. That is true, but He also knows what I'm going to pray for even before I ask, yet I am required to ask, anyway. It's in the asking that I express my trust in His covenant and the design in fellowship called prayer. If I had made such a list, it would have only included spiritual things. I probably would have started with my praying about an increase in personal holiness. That certainly seems like a safe place to start. From there I would probably move to the cry for a great number of souls saved. Praying for all the churches to grow to illustrate God's favor upon us to the world around us would also make this list. These prayers are very legitimate, and in reality are prayers I pray to this day. My mistake was in thinking that was all He cared about. I never would have confessed that, but it was the belief deeply hidden in my heart. And yet my discovery of His heart for me has changed my thinking completely. One of my richest discoveries about Him is *if it matters to me, it matters to Him.*

Today I have a growing list comprised of around 150 things that I would love to see Him fulfill. I keep the list in my iPad, so I can add to it at any moment of any day. But perhaps the most significant thing about my list is that I have natural things interwoven into my spiritual dreams. For example, I have on my list places in the world I would love to hunt or fish. And right after that, I might mention my cry to see cancer obliterated from our church family and eventually our city. And following that might be my desire to help my kids get better homes than they can naturally afford. The point is, I have found I don't think or see things like He does. And there are times He chooses to fulfill a natural dream before a spiritual, because it reveals His nature to me in ways I'd never learn otherwise.

One of the funnier examples of this is when I was looking through a fly-fishing catalogue one day. Fly-fishing is a favorite sport of mine, and I especially love to fish our local waters. Some of them are truly world-class. While looking through the catalogue, I stopped for a moment to look at unusual items on the last few pages. On one side of the page were a couple of flasks, right next to the crystal glasses and decanters. They were silver and looked very cool. A flask is something that some fly-fisherman use to put in brandy or whiskey and store it in their back pocket to drink during their day on the stream. I looked at it and saw the price was well within my means, but thought that as cool as it looks, I have no use for it. So it would be a waste of money for me to buy something I wouldn't use.

I was in the UK soon after this experience. A woman brought Beni and me each a gift. I had my wife open hers first. I don't remember exactly what it was now, but it was the kind of gift you'd give to a godly woman. When I opened mine, I was very surprised. It was a flask. I smiled and thanked her for such a wonderful gift. But in my heart I was thinking to God, "You've got to be kidding me! Do you realize how many critical items you passed over on my prayer list only to find a flask that wasn't even worth praying about?" It didn't even occupy the "it would be nice" or the "bonus" part of my prayer list.

That flask sits on my shelf to this day, unused. It is a daily reminder of a Father who watches every pause we take, every turning of the heart, every simple desire, watching over those things with delight.

I expect cancer to be healed when I pray. But why in the world would He have one of His dear ones spend money on something I have no use for? That flask is now priceless in value. It reveals the heart of a Father who is for me, which is an irreplaceable revelation. This was discovered in the fulfillment of a passing natural desire. It is an insight about His nature I never would have received simply through answering one of my big prayers.

If I'm going to contend for something in prayer, it's going to be for a healing, deliverance, the salvation of a soul—or perhaps the transformation of a city or nation. But I cannot ignore the fact that the One who is sovereign responded to a passing desire, to something as far removed from anything with eternal significance as can be imagined. But somehow, it has become one of the more spiritual moments of my life, as it brought me face to face with a Father who is Himself increasingly beyond all I could have possibly imagined or wanted.

My book of dreams has no structure or order. I have to keep it random to keep it fitting for the One who thinks and works completely differently than I. I am learning that He moves outside of my perception of what is important.

I read my list for inspiration. I pray over the dreams simply because I know He likes to hear me connect with Him about my desires. They bring Him pleasure. Our dreams become the real estate that God occupies as our delight and trust in Him increases.

BUILDING A LIFE WORTH ENJOYING

I'm easily drawn into things that have obvious eternal significance—souls, missions, healings and deliverances, all stir my heart like nothing else. But as previously stated, there is a seamless connection between the natural and the supernatural, and it's become vital for me to recognize and value the natural realm He longs to bless. Having said that, there is a concept that I once heard the great Bible teacher Bob Mumford speak on. He called it, "unstringing your bow." If you were to have an old-fashioned bow made of wood, you wouldn't want to keep the string on the bow all the time so that it was always prepared for use. Doing so would cause the bow to lose its strength, as the strength is found in the tension created by the wood that wants to remain stiff and straight. Bows that stay in the "taut condition," remaining ready to be used at all times, actually lose strength over time. So it is with us. Not knowing how, when, or with whom to relax has caused many an individual to burn out. I don't mean we are to relax spiritual standards or values. I mean physically, emotionally, and mentally, we must relax for the purpose of maintaining strength and obtaining total refreshing.

Consider the word recreation: *re-creation*. *Re* means "to go back" or "do again." While *creation* is the influence of His nature flowing through us where we are able to make creative contributions to our environment. Such is the purpose of recreation. It's not just mindless activity. It serves to restore us to original design and strength. Obviously, there are those who have made a god out of personal pleasure. As with everything, there's a right and wrong way of doing it. There are those who have found recreation to be a key in rebuilding their personal strength for the glory of God. Let us be the latter.

IT'S TIME TO PLAY

My favorite time in school was recess. I know there are those who loved the books and all the work. I just wasn't one of them. Not even for a day. Lessons were what I endured until it was time for recess or, later in life, Physical Education. In fact, my senior year in high school, I had enough credits in the last semester to be able to skip the study courses for most of the day and ended up with four P.E. classes—my kind of heaven. If they offered continual recesses or sports, I could have become a professional student.

All children love to play. We spend good money on a toy for our children or grandchildren to enjoy, and they spend the entire day playing in the box it came in. The box requires a bit more imagination and creativity to enjoy. Sometimes I think it would be cheaper and more fun if I just bought them blankets to drape over couches and tables to create their forts or, on occasion, a small city. It's called play. And children do it so well.

My personal assistant, Michael Van Tinteren, is a medical doctor from Australia. Recently he told me about a book he was reading about play, creativity, and performance. It's called *Free to Learn*, by author Peter Gray. The findings cited by the author are quite interesting and fun. For example:

> Learning, problem solving, and creativity are worsened by interventions that interfere with playfulness. But they are improved by the interventions that promote playfulness.
>
> In one…experiment, the researchers presented real physicians with a case history of a difficult-to-diagnose liver disease. The case included some misleading information, which created a barrier to identifying the relevant information and arriving at the correct solution. Mood manipulation was accomplished by giving some of the doctors a little bag of candy before presenting them with the problem…those who got the bag of candy arrived at the correct diagnosis more quickly than those who didn't. They reasoned more flexibly, took into account all of the information more readily, and were less likely to get stuck on false leads than were those who had not received candy.
>
> A "positive mood" improves creative, insightful reasoning… the particular type of positive mood that is most effective is a playful mood.
>
> In experiments conducted in England, M.G. Dias and P.L. Harris found that young children could solve logic problems in the context of play that they seemed unable to solve in a serious context.

...four-year-olds in play easily solved logic problems that they were not supposed to be able to solve until they were about ten or eleven years old. In fact, subsequent experiments showed that, to a lesser degree, even two-year-olds solved such problems when presented in a clearly playful manner.[5]

The art of play, fun, and joy is increasingly important to me and is essential in our culture. These were areas I shut down early in my walk with the Lord because I thought them to be unspiritual. But that changed many years ago for me, largely because I saw it didn't work. Not really. In that kind of *serious* atmosphere, there was little edification or zest for life in general.

Today I surround myself with people who really love life. They thrive as they love their families and people in general. Their joy of discovery and learning is huge. They inspire me. I have done my best to empower my team to become all that is in their hearts. And I am now better off because of what they've become. I heard one of our team members say recently, "I love us." Me, too.

FROM MY EXPERIENCE

I know I can't speak for anyone else, but in my experience, my intensity and focus in serving Jesus in some ways worked against what I was committed to do and become. It heightened my willingness to serve Him with obvious activities like prayer, fellowship, and giving. But it also heightened my awareness of myself. Such intensity didn't allow me to experience much joy outside of those events.

When I had the chance to look into the lives of personal heroes who were healthy in all aspects of life, I noticed they didn't look like me. The people I admired were also completely devoted to Jesus but seemed to be able to take delight in the simplest things in life. They were not at all materialistic, but were comfortable owning something nice, without apology. The peace that rested upon their lives existed without striving. These people thrived in the atmosphere of corporate worship, but were equally at home at a baseball game for their children. The point is, true spirituality is powerful, practical, natural, real, flexible, and uniquely satisfied in our own skin.

THE HEART OF THE FATHER

Our passion is to represent God well in every part of life. In doing so, we have worked to build a culture that celebrates the varieties found in life, the varieties of gifts in the people God has placed around us, and the great variety within His Church. Giving value to what He values is key for all things pertaining to the Kingdom of God.

We have determined to live a life that upholds and models His values. And in doing so, we have the privilege of building a culture where He is as at home here among us, as He is in Heaven. This is now our dream. We found it in the heart of God.

ADDENDUM

Chapter Seventeen

IMPROMPTU INTERVIEW

I often ask Pam Spinosi to help edit my writing. She's a great help in keeping the flow of information consistent. When I asked her to help me with this book, *The Way of Life*, she gave me a copy of this impromptu interview from December 2, 2015. I had forgotten all about it. This interview took place at a gathering with part of our staff at Bethel. It was not a planned interview, but someone had the presence of mind to record it. Pam transcribed it and made it available to our team. After reading it, I thought it might be helpful to you, the reader. There is a small amount of editing to make it more readable.

Kris: What is one thing that people might not know about you that you think would contribute to why the Lord has given you so much favor? What would you tell young people about the way you live that maybe isn't something you preach every week?

Bill: I don't know. I know this: that I don't have a hidden agenda when I have a relationship with somebody.

Kris: That's good. What about your relationship with God?

Bill: In my relationship with the Lord, faithfulness is my supreme value. I don't have anything that's more important to me than that.

Kris: What does faithfulness mean to you? I know that it means more than most people think by watching your life. What does that mean to you?

Bill: My key verse since 1972 has been Proverbs 4:29: *"Watch over your heart with all diligence, for out of it flow the issues of life."* I monitor my attitude and values. I don't do introspection. (Well, I mean, I do it very well, actually. I try not to do it, as it ends up in disaster. So I don't do that.) But I do try to monitor attitude and values—that is what's important to me.

Kris: The way you process conflict or a problem with a person who is not behaving well, how does that relate to your value for faithfulness? I have seen people mess up, but the way that you respond to that is one of the unique things about who you are and about our culture. What creates that in you that you respond quite differently from most people?

Bill: It's hard to reject someone you know. It's easy to reject someone you read about in the paper. It's that personal relationship that makes the difference. So, if I am in the room with somebody, I am going to generally respond to them differently than if it were just a report that I heard. It may sound a little strange, but what I feel like I have a responsibility to do is to try to know the person who is not in the room. In other words, in some way to have a personal engagement with them even though I don't know them or may have never met them.

Kris: It's like that benefit-of-the-doubt attitude that kind of flows out of you all the time, where you don't know the other side of the story. There is always something working inside your mind like, "It may not be exactly the way it looks," right?

Bill: It hardly ever is the way it looks. I've made the mistake like everyone of coming to a conclusion without all the information. It's so easy to come to conclusions too quickly. And it's really tough to take a conclusion back. It's really tough. It's tough to recover from a bad conclusion. You can be forgiven, but it's hard to undo the words.

Kris: You are famous for believing in people nobody else believes in. And that's coming from the way you view life, right? Is it coming from that desire to watch over your heart?

Bill: Yeah, I think so. I think the bottom line is how would I want to be treated? You are planting seeds when there are premature judgments and premature conclusions. And those are the kinds of seeds you will have to harvest later. They are not fun at all, so I try to watch that. I don't do it perfectly, but I work hard to watch that.

Tom: When you say you watch over your heart, what does that look like for you? Do you have indicators you are looking for like, "I need to step back there"? What's that look like to you?

Bill: Attitude. Impatience. Harshness. Confrontational in an unhealthy way. All of those kinds of things can stir up indifference toward somebody. They create distance, which becomes easier if I avoid someone. Any of those kinds of things are indicators. If I spot those things going on in me, then I take that as a warning.

Tom: So if you feel impatient with somebody, frustrated, that's your indicator to back up?

Bill: It's a sign for me to be careful. I need to take charge over whatever is causing that. What is it? Impatience? That often comes from the need to be in control. The bottom line of the need to be in control is the absence of trust in God. So I have to step back and cultivate that trust.

Kris: The other thing that you do probably better than anybody that I know is to allow other people to get big around you, and I would imagine you have the same human emotions at times like jealousy or any of those kinds of synonyms. How are you dealing with those things, so that when they come up, it doesn't become a culture where you need to make someone small or reduce them? Or give them any kind of a lid? You don't do that. I know you don't do that. Everyone in this room knows you don't do that. That is polar opposite from probably most every other culture we see. What are you doing inside to make sure the right thing happens?

Bill: I really want people to succeed! I really do! I want people to become everything God made them to become. I mean that is a legitimate desire. And I do have a certain realization that that is not necessarily dependent on me. I have a role. I get to influence, I get to fan the flame or whatever. But if I think it's dependent on me, then I'm going to somehow try to control the destiny. But I realize I get to contribute to it, and the measure that I contribute to one person will be different than another. It's going to be according to the relationship, according to the time I have with them. But I want them to succeed, and I know that God has put something in them. And I can tell you, I have, on several occasions, feared the person. They may be small in title and everything, but I have feared God in them in a right way. The Scriptures tell us to "Submit to one another in the fear of Christ." I've actually looked at a person, and realized, God is doing something here. They are far from perfect, but I had better not mess this up, and I had better give them room to grow.

Jordan: When I interact with you, the sense I always get is this man is so intimate with the Lord; he's a friend of the Lord. If we want to be friends with the Lord, what would you advise us to do to position ourselves now?

Bill: Grow in your affection for Him, and stop evaluating yourself. Just get over yourself. Just the affection, the adoration, it's the willingness to spend time without asking for anything. So I'll have extended prayer times and never pray for anything.

Tom: How is getting over yourself connected to friendship with the Lord?

Bill: If you are constantly evaluating yourself, you're not going to ever feel qualified for that friendship because you will live with this awareness of what doesn't work, what's not right. You just always disqualify yourself. When there is constant evaluation of how I'm doing, somehow I'm going to end up disqualifying myself. Not disqualifying myself as a believer or a follower or loved by God. Not that. It hasn't gotten to that. But you end up disqualifying yourself for the significance that He has for you. So it just comes down to being impressed with His significance over your own insignificance. One has to stand out stronger than the other. And it makes up for what you feel you lack. I live with awareness of what I lack. I don't know that you ever escape that. But grace means that He more than makes up for the lack.

Kris: Is it good to live with a certain amount of awareness of your lack? Is that a positive thing?

Bill: Probably. I don't like it, but I think it helps in being poor in spirit. But the problem is that it gets overused to where you start discrediting yourself, diminishing your worth. The need for courage sometimes is in the instant, and if you've been devaluing yourself, that courage in the instant isn't there. You may be able to come to it. But some situations need it in an instant. And to have that, you've got to have that abiding sense of not only acceptance but of celebration from the Father. And then that courage can be instant. When you live reading what these great people did and what those great people did, and you see what you do or what you lack, you know, you just discredit yourself. It's just not healthy. When you evaluate yourself, there is a constant pressure to accomplish something in prayer instead of just to be with Him.

Tom: It makes you come to prayer with an agenda.

Bill: Yeah, which He doesn't mind. He'll meet with you for anything. He'll meet with you about complaints. But the issue is to develop that sense of presence. I don't think it should be connected to an agenda or an assignment. Assignments are right, and He manifests Himself on us because of specific assignments, so I realize that. Whenever He said, "I will be with you," it's because He had just given the apostles an assignment, so there is a connection there. But I think the whole root system of that lifestyle is an adoration, an affection that is not connected to any performance, any assignment, any title, any success or any failure.

Chris: I've watched you for 15 years. Your life has just inspired me so much. I have seen you come in from trips, and you're at the office before 6 a.m., praying on Sunday mornings. You're there. You could have just come in on Saturday night, and you're there every Sunday. How do you prepare? What is it like before a message? What do you do to prepare because every message that you deliver is *boom!* I don't see outlines. It's different. How do you go about preparing a message? How do you put the thoughts together? Is it something you've been chewing on all week? Is it a message that the Lord's been speaking to you about?

Bill: It's probably all the above. Sometimes He drops a seed into my heart, and it develops over a period of years. I actually did a series on wisdom a year ago that had been growing for ten years. Sometimes He drops a seed that morning. There is no consistency except that for me to prepare my heart means that I come to Him in adoration first. I don't come with a need for a message. I come in adoration out of desire to be with Him. And I would rather have nothing to say and be current in my fellowship with Him than to have lots to say and be trying to find Him. That's the main thing for me is I make sure that I am current…that my relationship is fresh. It's about feeling His pleasure, which is the awareness of His heart.

Sometimes I see a big picture, and I can feel it strong. Sometimes I'm just looking for anything that His heart is on, and I know it here, but to have that sense of His heartbeat for something. The King James Version of Hebrews 11 means a lot to me because it helped me with something. It said, "Faith is the conviction of things hoped for." Anything that's apart from faith is sin. So that means I have to look. I look at a whole gamut of subjects, and I have to notice, "All right. This is where my heart is burning. This is where I have conviction." So I know if I have conviction for something, then I know I'll have faith for it. When you're ministering out of faith, it is impartable. This is not just knowledge or an inspiring word or something to encourage people with, as valuable as that is. There is actually substance on it that can change people's lives. So I look for where there's conviction.

I even try to follow that example in a prayer line when there are 100 people to pray for. I'll look through the line and see where I can feel a conviction. I don't know what the person's problem is, and I don't know what's going on, but I can feel a conviction. I'll follow that. Paul said you're restricted by your affections, so I look for where my affections are. Affection is conviction to me. "Moved with compassion" is the same subject. I'll look to where something is ignited, and I'll follow that. As long as I stay with that, I do pretty well. When I start to run outside of where I have conviction, I fatigue a lot faster. It can still work, but I fatigue so much faster.

Chris: Bill, when did it start for you, developing this close connection to the Lord? Was there a defining moment? I know you talk about the baptism of the Holy Spirit, where like the lightening just came. You were asking God for the more and then God gave you an encounter at night, but were there other things prior to that where you were just, "God, I want to live like this for the rest of my life"?

Bill: Well, my big yes to the Lord came in the same season; it was immediately followed by the season when my dad began to teach on worship. And I think it was after the second or third message, I remember (if the building were still there, I think I could show you close to where I sat at that particular message) I bowed my head at the end of the message and said, "God, I give you the rest of my life to teach me that one thing." There wasn't an altar call. It wasn't that kind of a message. It was just I knew I heard why I was alive. So I prayed a prayer on that Sunday morning: "I give you the rest of my life to teach me this one thing—to know what it is to minister to you." And that means you have to be a presence-based person. So it's not a performance, obviously. It's not necessarily tied to music, although that's a pretty integral part of it. It's more of a heart surrender, where you are drawn by affection. You are drawn by adoration. So I would say it started right at the beginning. It really did. There are layers to everything, so He intensifies it. You put all your chips in the middle of the table, and you get a winning hand. Then you have more to put in the middle of the table. That's kind of the way it is. You give Him everything. Then you experience increase, and you have to give Him everything again. It's that cycle that really is our life. I said yes to everything. I'll do anything. I'll go anywhere. I don't ever have to own anything. It doesn't matter to me. Then He gives you increase, and you have to do it all over again. That's the ongoing cycle.

Shara: Are there practical things you do to guard that intimacy, that friendship, that adoration? Even time-wise?

Bill: Well, time is a challenge. I think it helps not to evaluate the size of your assignment (personal title). Otherwise, you might get impressed with it. It's not healthy. I don't ever want to measure myself by my responsibilities. I'm no bigger than my affection.

Joaquin: Can you talk about following the affection of your heart not only in reference to preparing for a message, but it feels like you use that as a guiding force in leading, too. In everything you do, when problems show up, how do you lead from that place of following the affection of your heart?

Bill: Are you talking about affection for God or for people?

Joaquin: I think, for God.

Bill: Well, if I am leading people, then my affection for God has me fear God in people and realize that I have a responsibility to treasure what He values, and that's people. There is a real caution over misuse of authority, position, responsibility, any of those things, to somehow have personal gain at the expense of another person. That's just frightening. That's terrible. So that sense of adoration helps, I think, to make sure that you lead people for their sake, not yours.

Joaquin: It seems like you make decisions as a leader in stewarding the church different than a lot of people would make decisions, and you're not swayed as much by the natural, but it's like always going back to "What's the affection of my heart?" Chris asked in preparing for a sermon, and you're talking about following the affection of your heart when you're praying for somebody in the prayer line, but in the bigger picture, leading a movement, how do you follow that?

Bill: I don't know. I don't know that it would be any different. I know there's a movement, and I know I— and we together—have this responsibility, but to be honest, I don't ever think about it. I think there are people who are gifted to live with an awareness of what and who is following. I don't live with that awareness, and I don't think it's because of spirituality. I just think it's because of my bent in seeing. I think I am wired to see the moves of the wind. That's what I think I'm wired to see. Other giftings are more inclined to pick up, "All right. We have responsibility here. We have responsibility there. This group is following. We need to make contribution here." I think there is great wisdom in it. And I would never suggest that my perspective is better or more spiritual because I don't think it is. But the way I'm wired is that's not important to me. It really isn't. What's important to me is where He's going.

Kris: But in another sense, you value people for whom that *is* important.

Bill: Oh, I do. To be honest, I succeed because of their gift. I'm so thankful that there are people who are wired that way because I'd have to fake it to do it well, and it would pull me out of what I do well. I have only got a couple things that I really do well. So I give myself to that, and I come to a place of

peace where I'm OK with just spending my life doing what my heart burns for, and then raising up
and empowering people who carry the rest of it.
That's so helpful for me because we would have
only 10 percent of what we have now if it was dependent on my gift.

Chapter Eighteen

THE VALUES THAT DEFINE US

E arlier in this book, I addressed the four cornerstones of thought that reveal our heart and purpose. They are just that for us—cornerstones that set a foundation, boundaries, and values for how we do life in our attempt to shape the course of world history. But the list of values we have been called to emphasize is far greater. Dann Farrelly, one of my associates and Dean of Students for Bethel School of Supernatural Ministry, wrote the following in his wonderful book, *Kingdom Culture*. It is a fascinating and much more complete list of the values that motivate us. It is these truths that work to reveal our purpose and destiny. Following each paragraph is the scriptural basis for these statements, for those who would like to go deeper.

GOD IS GOOD

God describes Himself as gracious and compassionate, slow to anger and abounding in love. He is good and, by nature, in a good mood.

The message, ministry, and sacrifice of Jesus perfectly reveal the nature of God as a good Father. He is for us and chose to redeem us from sin. We cannot do whatever we want and expect God to always bless us. Even that is because He is a good Father. He remains the ultimate judge of every human being, and we can trust Him regardless of our circumstances. The life of a believer is not free from trials or persecution. But, while enemies come to steal and kill, we know that Jesus came to destroy demonic works and give us authority and abundant life. God's goodness is extravagant and we are His masterpiece. As we remember and retell what He has done through our testimonies, faith is created as He is able and eager to do it again.

> **Study:** Psalm 103:8-13; Acts 14:16-17; James 1:17-18; 2 Peter 3:9; Matthew 7:11; Galatians 5:22-23; Psalm 119:68; Zephaniah 3:17; Psalm 104; Exodus 34:5-7; Acts 17:22-31; John 3:16-17; Hebrews 1:2-3; John 14:6-7; Isaiah 9:6; Colossians 1:19, 2:9; John 1:1,18; 8:1-11,19; Romans 8:28-32; Hebrews 11:6; Nahum 1:7; James 1:12-18; Matthew 10:29-31; Acts 16:23-26; John 10:10-11; 1 John 3:8; Acts 10:38; 1 Peter 5:8-10; Ephesians 6:12; Mark 5:1-19; Romans 10:15-17; Hebrews 13:7-8; Acts 10:34-48; Revelation 19:10; Psalm 44:1-5; 119:11; Mark 5:18-21; Deuteronomy 6:17-24; 1 Chronicles 16:23-36; Joshua 4:1-9

SALVATION CREATES JOYFUL IDENTITY

Jesus has won absolute victory! We are forgiven and freed from the enemy's power of sin, sickness, lies, and torment. While we feel godly conviction when we sin, we no longer live under shame or condemnation. We live in the power of righteousness, healing, truth, and joy. We are adopted as royalty into God's family and are commanded to help others be reconciled to God our Father. We have been given authority and access to God's resources for the sake of our victory and for the sake of touching the world with the Gospel. We are simultaneously joyful servants, trusted friends, and beloved children of our Lord. We are new creations, not merely sinners saved by grace but saints who have been given His righteousness so we can partner with God our Father.

> **Study:** Romans 8:1-4; 2 Corinthians 5:17; Romans 6:4; Galatians 2:20; Hebrews 2:14-15; Galatians 5:22-24; 1 Corinthians 15:56-57; Revelation 1:12-18; Romans 8:14-17; John 1:12; 2 Corinthians 5:18-21; 1 Peter 2:9; 1 John 3:1; Luke 15:11-32; John 15:12-15; Psalm 16:11; Hebrews 1:9; 12:2; Matthew 25:23; Psalm 100:2; Galatians 1:10; Matthew 23:11-12; John 1:12; 1 John 3:1; Matthew 25:14-30; 2 Corinthians 5:17-21; 1 Corinthians 1:30; Romans 3:21-26; 8:1,30; Galatians 2:19-20; Acts 26

RESPONSIVE TO GRACE

We joyfully experience the astounding, undeserved love of God and His ongoing power to transform us. Our old self is dead—crucified with Christ. We are now free and empowered to live in His righteousness and share in His sufferings. None of us has attained perfection, but His transforming love and power are inseparable from one another. God scandalously loves His lost creation and extends grace to us, enabling believers to love Him and others at a higher standard than the law. Deeply experiencing grace teaches us about righteousness, which equips us to overcome sin and failure. The Father's love keeps us from focusing on sin or hiding in shame if we fail. His grace breaks the mentality that says "I am a powerless victim of circumstances" and creates a new identity that declares, "In Christ, I am a victorious overcomer, no matter the situation." We choose daily to live in the fullness of His abundant grace.

> **Study:** John 3:16-17; Ephesians 1:4-5; 2:8-10; Romans 5:6-11; Mark 5:1-20; Romans 5:7-8; 2 Corinthians 5:14-18; Romans 6:11-14; Matthew 5:21-28; Romans 8:2-4; Acts 9:1-22; 26:1-23; Ephesians 3:14-21; 2 Corinthians 3:17-18; Titus 2:11-13; Colossians 3:1-5; Acts 2:14-41; John 16:33; 1 John 4:4; Romans 8:31-32,35-39; 1 Corinthians 15:57; 2 Corinthians 2:14; Deuteronomy 28:13; Jeremiah 29:11

FOCUSED ON HIS PRESENCE

Our first ministry is to God. He has made us a dwelling place for His Spirit. As we behold Him, we are moved to worship with joyous passion. God delights in us and He has always desired to be with us. We focus on His presence because we have discovered that He is focused on us. Being focused on His presence doesn't mean Christians should spend all their time in private worship, though. Purposefully cultivating a hunger for God's manifest presence and an openness to experiencing the Holy Spirit deepens our friendship with God and our awareness that we carry His presence for the sake of the world. Every part of a Christian's life is sacred and meant to be holy. We do not live with the false mindset that life is divided into the "sacred" or the "secular." Rather, God is involved in and valued in every area of our lives. The Holy Spirit lives in us, so everything we do and everywhere we go is sacred. As a lifestyle, we practice recognizing God's presence while we minister to others, attempting to say what He is saying and do what He is doing.

> **Study:** Psalm 27:4; Luke 10:39-42; James 4:8; Psalm 1:1-3; 23:6; 26:8; John 4:23; Psalm 22:3; Ephesians 1:4-5; Zephaniah 3:17; Jeremiah 31:3; Psalm 65:4; 1 John 3:1; Revelation 3:20; 1 John 4:19; Psalm 73:28; 107:9; John 1:16; Matthew 5:6; Isaiah 55:1-2; 1 Corinthians 3:16; John 5:19-20,30; 12:49-50; 14:10; 1 John 4:16-17

CREATING HEALTHY FAMILY

We are adopted into God's family, so we intentionally create family and community wherever we go. The way we love people is a direct reflection of our love for God. So, we think like healthy family members and do what's best for the whole environment, mutually submitting to one another in love and unselfishness. In covenant relationships, we purposely grow our capacity to trust and be trusted as we empower and confront one another in order to live out who we truly are. We are loyal, which is demonstrated most radically when people fail. Forgiveness is our standard and everyone is given the opportunity to rebuild trust in the community. We do not punish and abandon those who fail in order to save face or show we hate sin, but instead we commit to helping them be restored.

> **Study:** Ephesians 1:5; 2:19; Matthew 12:48-50; Galatians 6:10; Romans 8:15-16; 1 Peter 2:17; Acts 2:41-47; Philippians 2:3; Romans 12:9-21; Ephesians 5:21; Galatians 5:13; 1 Corinthians 13; Ruth 1:16-17; Matthew 18:15; Luke 17:3-4; Ephesians 4:15-16; 1 Corinthians 4:14-21; 1 Thessalonians 5:14; 1 Samuel 20; Galatians 6:1; Matthew 18:15; John 8:1-11; Psalm 141:5; John 21

GOD'S WORD TRANSFORMS

The goal of Scripture is to bring us into a relationship with the Author and transform us into His likeness. The Bible should lead us into an ever-growing relationship with the Father, Son, and Holy Spirit. As God brings us into encounters with Him through His Word, faith is released into our lives. God is never boxed in by our current understanding of His Word, but studying His truth empowers us to believe in who He is, who we are, and how He wants us to live. The primary lens through which we interpret the Bible is the person, life, and redemptive work of Jesus, because He is the most complete revelation of who God is and what He cares about. The Bible is the source of infallible truth and authority by which we judge all insight and prophetic revelation. Studying the Word and experiencing God's presence should never be separated from one another. His Word is alive and, when we declare it, we partner with Him to transform the world.

> **Study:** John 5:39-40; 2 Timothy 3:15-17; Matthew 4:4;
> 2 Corinthians 3:15-18; James 1:22-25; Ephesians 5:25-27;
> Psalm 119:11; Luke 24:13-35 Romans 10:17; 1 Thessalonians 2:13; John 17:17; Matthew 7:24-28; Colossians 3:15-17;
> John 8:31-32; Psalm 119:105; Romans 15:4; 1 Corinthians
> 10:1-13; Acts 8:26-40; John 5:37-47; Luke 24:25-32; John
> 1:14; 14:9-11; Colossians 1:15-20; 2:9; Hebrews 1:1-3; 2 Peter
> 1:16-21; 2 Timothy 3:15-17; Matthew 22:29; John 8:31-32;
> 2 Thessalonians 2:13-15; 2 Peter 1:16-21; Proverbs 30:5-6;
> Psalm 119:160; Matthew 4:1-11

GOD'S STILL SPEAKING

God wants to communicate with His family. It is important for us to actively listen for His voice and experience the variety of ways He communicates. Scripture calls us to earnestly desire the gift of prophecy, which is to speak on God's behalf to strengthen, encourage, and comfort people. We desire to say what the Father is saying to help people grow in their identity and discover their God-given purpose and value. Prophecy is not one-way communication. It involves two people hearing from God—the one who gives the prophetic word and the one who receives it. While God is perfect, He has chosen to partner with imperfect people to build His Kingdom. With the Holy Spirit, Scripture, and our community, we judge the spirit and accuracy of the words we give and receive. Holding on to what is good, we let go of what is not. The Bible is the ultimate, authoritative revelation unlike any other; nothing will be added to it. Therefore, prophecy should never contradict properly interpreted Scripture.

> **Study:** John 10:26-28; 16:13; Matthew 4:4; Isaiah 50:4-5; 1 John 2:27; Acts 2:17; Numbers 11:29; 1 Kings 19:9-13; 1 Corinthians 14:1-4; John 12:49; 1 Timothy 4:14-16; Acts 2:17; 1 Corinthians 14:24-25; Acts 13:1-3; 1 Thessalonians 5:19-22; 1 Corinthians 14:29; Luke 9:55; Acts 21:10-22:24; 27:10,22-24; Galatians 1:6-9; 2 Timothy 3:16-17; 2 Thessalonians 2:13-15; Matthew 7:15-20; John 8:31-32; 2 Peter 1:16-21

JESUS EMPOWERS SUPERNATURAL MINISTRY

Jesus promised signs would follow believers and they would do even greater works than He did. Miracles did not stop with Jesus and the apostles. Because of this, we owe the world an opportunity to experience the power of God and an invitation to salvation because Jesus sent us into the world, just as the Father sent Him, with the power of the Holy Spirit. Nothing is impossible with God. We do not pursue a relationship with God just so we can perform signs and wonders. The Holy Spirit gives every believer the supernatural power to witness and release miracles, signs, and wonders, and it is our responsibility to represent the heart of the Father well. Therefore, no person or situation is beyond His ability to bring complete restoration. We believe all can be healed because Jesus demonstrated the Father's will in healing all the sick and demonized He encountered. Above all, love should be our motivation when we take risks to release the power of God's Kingdom in to the lives of others.

> **Study:** John 14:12-14; Acts 2:17-18; Luke 9:1-2; Mark 16:15-18; Acts 5:12-16; John 20:21-23; 1 Corinthians 2:4-5;

John 17:18; 1 Thessalonians 1:5; Matthew 28:18-19; 5:14-16; Luke 10:1-9; Matthew 17:20; Mark 10:25-27; John 15:7; 1 Corinthians 6:9-11; Psalm 103:1-7; Luke 1:34-37; Matthew 4:23; 12:15; 14:14; 24-33; Luke 9:11; Acts 10:38; Psalm 103:3-4; Acts 3:1-10; James 2:14-18; Mark 10:46-52; Matthew 9:27-38

HIS KINGDOM IS ADVANCING

God is big and victorious. The devil is small and defeated. We are in a battle, but the outcome is not in doubt! We focus on the good that God is doing in the world and, even though we do not deny the existence of difficult or painful circumstances, we live with contagious hope and joy. We believe and live the prayer, *"Your Kingdom come, Your will be done on earth as it is in heaven."* Therefore, we partner with the King in natural and supernatural ways to establish mercy, justice, and righteousness until He comes. As believers, we are all in full-time ministry as God advances His Kingdom into every area of society. Our work and efforts both inside and outside the church are sacred and valuable acts of worship to God. Although we will experience resistance and conflict as the Kingdom advances, we expect the culture to be changed as people come to salvation and take their places in God's purpose for the world. We live to make the world better for generations that we will never see.

Study: 1 John 4:4; Colossians 2:13-15; 1 John 2:13; 5:4-5; Romans 8:31-39; John 12:31; Acts 4:23-31; 1 John 3:8; Hebrews 2:14-15; John 16:33; Mark 5:1-13; Matthew 6:9-10; 10:7-8; Isaiah 9:7; 33:5-6; Micah 6:8; Matthew 10:42; 25:40; John 14:12; James 1:27; Matthew 12:22-29; 1 Peter 2:9; Romans 12:1; Matthew 5:13-16; Colossians 3:23-24; Daniel 6:3; Proverbs 22:29; Ephesians 6:5-9; Matthew 25:31-46; John 15:19-21; 16:33; Colossians 1:13-14; 2 Corinthians

> 4:8-11; 12:10; Nehemiah 2:1-10; Matthew 5:13-16; Acts 19:11-41

FREE AND RESPONSIBLE

Christ died to set us free from sin, death, fear, guilt, and shame in order to establish us in freedom so we can live and love as God's glorious children. Environments of freedom, responsibility, and empowerment enable people to live holy, healthy, bold, creative lives. While freedom is very personal, it is not self-centered. In our freedom, we still live a life that is submitted to the Lord. Our freedom is not the ability to do whatever we want, but instead it is the ability to do what is right. We have been given freedom so we may present ourselves to the Lord as a willing sacrifice, surrendered and ready to serve. Freedom and responsibility are inseparable. We experience true freedom as we cooperate with the Holy Spirit to produce the fruit of self-control and use our freedom to bless others. It is not our goal to remove sinful choices from people, but instead call them to freely love God and choose His righteousness. We are responsible for partnering with the Holy Spirit to continually develop the foundation of our character so our character can support our growing influence and anointing.

> **Study:** Romans 8:1-2; 15-21; Galatians 5:1; Romans 6:4,14-22; 2 Corinthians 3:17; 5:17; 1 John 4:17-18; Luke 19:1-10; Galatians 5:13-14; Romans 12:1-2; 14:7-9; 15:1-7; Matthew 4:1-11; Galatians 5:13-25; 1 Corinthians 9:19; 2 Peter 1:5-9; 1 Corinthians 8:9-13; 1 Peter 1:13-16; John 13:12-17; 2 Peter 1:5-9; Titus 2:11-12; Ephesians 4:1; Colossians 1:10; 1 Corinthians 6:18-20; Luke 9:54-56

HONOR AFFIRMS VALUE

Honor recognizes and affirms that every person is valuable and powerful. We are made in God's image. He died to restore us to relationship with Him; therefore, we are significant. Though we are all equally loved by God, we are not equally empowered by God or the community. In spite of our differences, honor recognizes and celebrates the best in people, knowing that the level of honor we have for a person directly affects our ability to receive from them. We do not have to agree with everyone, but we respond to people based on their God-given identity and the honor in our hearts, not their behavior or self-definition. This means that we love people even if we do not receive anything from them in return. Honor is demonstrated through consistent respect in word and action toward those we lead, follow, love, and disagree with. While honor avoids controlling others, it also lovingly confronts, limits, and disciplines when necessary.

Study: Genesis 1:26-28; Ephesians 4:23-24; Psalm 139:13-16; Romans 12:10; 1 Corinthians 12:14-26; 1 Peter 2:17; Matthew 26:6-13; 1 Corinthians 12:14-26; 2 Corinthians 5:16-17; James 2:1-5; Philippians 2:3; 1 Samuel 24:1-10; 1 Corinthians 13:1-7; Leviticus 19:15-18; Galatians 6:1-2; Ephesians 4:14-15; Romans 2:4; Matthew 18:15; Hebrews 12:11-14; 2 Timothy 3:16-17; Luke 3:10-14; Matthew 10:40-42; Philippians 2:1-4; 1 Corinthians 4:14-20; 2 Kings 4:8-37

GENEROUS LIKE MY FATHER

God is extravagantly generous, and our generosity is a response and reflection of His nature. He is a good Father who gives good gifts to His children. The thread of God's generosity weaves through His creation, covenants, Israel's economics, the Gospel, and the Kingdom as

He consistently models that it is more blessed to give than to receive. While being rich or poor is neither a virtue nor a sin, God has blessed us so that we can be generous in every way to advance the Gospel. Joyfully giving our time, affection, talents, and money attracts God's attention, draws Heaven's blessing, produces transformation, and enables Him to trust us with the true riches of the Kingdom. Generosity is a form of honor. It confronts our poverty mindsets while changing the way we interact with the world. No longer anxious because we mistakenly believe provision is scarce, we are confident that God multiplies resources and is eager to rescue and prosper people. Generosity releases joy, blessing, and favor into our lives. As we give, it will be given to us, pressed down, shaken together, and running over!

> **Study:** James 1:17; Psalm 103:1-5; John 3:16; Ephesians 1:3; 2 Corinthians 8:9; 9:8; Acts 14:17; Matthew 7:7-11; Luke 15:11-32; Psalm 65:9-13; Deuteronomy 28:1-14; 7:9; 2 Corinthians 8:9; Matthew 20:28; Ephesians 1:3,7-8; James 1:5; Acts 20:35; Mark 12:41-43; 2 Corinthians 9:6-15; Acts 10:3-6; Malachi 3:10-12; Deuteronomy 8:18; Acts 2:43-47; Matthew 10:7-8; Luke 16:10-13; Acts 4:32-37; 2 Corinthians 9:6-15; Philippians 4:19; Ephesians 3:20-21; 1 Kings 17:10-16; 2 Kings 4:1-7; 3 John 2; Matthew 6:25-34; Jeremiah 29:11; Deuteronomy 28:11-13; Exodus 3:8; Matthew 14:13-21; Luke 6:38; Isaiah 58:6-12; Proverbs 11:25; Acts 2:43-47; Philippians 4:17-19; 1 Timothy 6:17-19; Luke 18:29-30; 19:1-10

HOPE IN A GLORIOUS BRIDE

The Church is the Bride of Christ, and she will successfully fulfill His great commission to make disciples of all nations. That means the nations will experience transformation. We work to leave a legacy and an inheritance for future generations, just as previous generations have done for us. While anticipating Christ's glorious return, we simply do not know when He will come, which should inspire us to have a long-term earthly vision. We are called to be the light of the world, not the light of the Church. So, we are looking not to escape the world, but to see Christ's victory manifested in individuals and nations, even in the face of resistance and conflict. The Church is called to overcome in all circumstances—in times of suffering and persecution, but also in times of prosperity and great influence.

Study: Ephesians 5:25-27; Matthew 28:16-20; Acts 1:8; Psalm 2:8; Revelation 11:15; Isaiah 54:3-5; 60:1-5; Acts 2; Proverbs 13:22; Acts 2:39; 2 Timothy 2:1-2; Titus 2:11-14; James 5:7-8; Isaiah 9:6-7; Matthew 25:1-29; Hebrews 11:4-30; John 17:15-18; Luke 10:2-3; Matthew 28:18-19; Hebrews 12:1-3; John 16:33; Revelation 11:15; Acts 13:13-52; John 16:33; Revelation 3:5,21; Philippians 4:11-13; Isaiah 41:10; 1 John 4:4; 5:4; Romans 8:37-39; 1 Chronicles 28:6-10; 1 Kings 5:3-5; Acts 4:13-37

NOTES

1. This subject is dealt with much more completely in Chapter 2 of my book, *When Heaven Invades Earth*, Destiny Image Publishing.

2. This is an edited version of what is in Chapter One of my book *God Is Good*.

3. This subject is dealt with much more thoroughly in my books *Dreaming with God* and *The Power that Changes the World*.

4. This section was adapted from my book, *The Power that Changes the World*, with Chosen Books. Used by permission.

5. Peter Gray, *Free to Learn: Why Unleashing the Instinct to Play Will Make Our Children Happier, More Self-Reliant, and Better Students for Life* (New York: Basic Books, 2013), 132-139.

About Bill Johnson

Bill Johnson is a fifth-generation pastor with a rich heritage in the Holy Spirit. Bill and his wife, Beni, are the senior leaders of Bethel Church in Redding, California, and serve a growing number of churches that cross denominational lines, demonstrate power, and partner for revival. Bill's vision is for all believers to experience God's presence and operate in the miraculous—as expressed in his bestselling books *When Heaven Invades Earth* and *Hosting the Presence*. The Johnsons have three children and ten grandchildren.

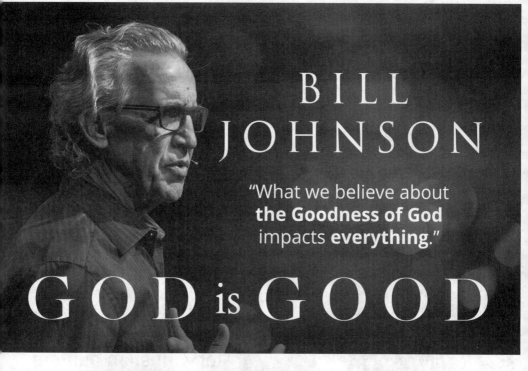
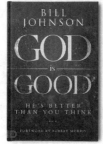